The Potter's Studio

CLAY & GLAZE

HANDBOOK

QUARRY

This book is dedicated to Jared Branfman,
a young potter who had great energy and talent.
I am saddened by the loss of such promise.

—J.Z.

Wood-fired cup
by Jared Branfman

First published in the United States of America by
Quarry Books, a member of
Quayside Publishing Group
100 Cummings Center
Suite 406-L
Beverly, Massachusetts 01915-6101
Telephone: (978) 282-9590
Fax: (978) 283-2742
www.quarrybooks.com

Library of Congress Cataloging-in-Publication Data

Zamek, Jeff.
  The potter's studio clay and glaze handbook : an essential guide to choosing, working, and designing with clay and glaze in the ceramic studio / Jeff Zamek.
     p. cm.
  Includes index.
  ISBN-13: 978-1-59253-522-4
  ISBN-10: 1-59253-522-4
  1. Pottery craft—Handbooks, manuals, etc. 2. Pottery craft—Equipment and supplies—Handbooks, manuals, etc. I. Title.
  TT919.5.Z36 2009
  738.1'42—dc22

                                        2008046367

ISBN-13: 978-1-59253-522-4
ISBN-10: 1-59253-522-4

10 9 8 7 6 5 4 3 2 1

Cover Design: Sandra Salamony
Spread Design: 4 Eyes Design
Additional Spread Design and Layout: Leslie Haimes

Photography: Randy O'Rourke, pages 22, 28, 30, 32, 33, 37 (bottom), 39, 40, 42, 46, 47, 51, 56, 59, 62, 63, 64 (bottom), 65, 69, 70, 73, 79, 82, 83, 87, 91, 103, 105, 107, 113, 116 (right), 129, 130, 132, 135 (bottom), 136 (top), 137 (top), 141, and 142.
Printed in Singapore

Special thanks to The Artisan Gallery of Northampton, MA, for the location photography.

Note: It is industry-standard for many clay and glaze formulations to be given in metric.

The Potter's Studio

CLAY & GLAZE

HANDBOOK

Jeff Zamek

BEVERLY MASSACHUSETTS

QUARRY BOOKS

An Essential Guide to Choosing, Working, and Designing with Clay and Glaze in the Ceramic Studio

CONTENTS

INTRODUCTION

As we all know, potters have patience and persistence. It is a required tool for working with quixotic clay, glazes, and kilns. How many of your plates have cracked during bisque firing? Remember when your favorite glaze ran off the pot onto the kiln shelf? With every pot you create, every bowl you throw, and every mug you glaze, you negotiate a vast set of variables that ultimately determine whether the product is a keeper or a throw-away. (I like to say those are the pots with character.) Over time, as you practice your craft, your pots begin to reflect your growing experience.

There's no fast-forward in pottery. You can't race from beginner to professional, and inevitably, as you advance, you will get stuck at some point along the way. Some potters get stuck at the stage of manipulating raw materials while trying to produce their own glazes and clay body formulas; others get stuck at the kiln firing stage, when they are incapable of firing a gas, wood, or electric kiln successfully; and still others get stuck at differing points. Take comfort in knowing that everyone gets stuck at some point.

In the beginning and intermediate stages of making pots, you quickly master skills and techniques. Every week reveals a better bowl or a bigger plate. You see significant improvements literally from one pot to the next. As you gain experience, such dramatic leaps in technique become less evident. You embark on a slow evolution, noting slight changes in glaze design or the subtle change of a bowl lip, but not realizing significant improvements like you did in the past. The magic of going from a ball of clay to a bowl fades to frustration when glazes crack or pots form with uneven walls.

At this stage, the work shifts from becoming less a technical mastery of clay and glazes to a personal statement expressed through the clay and glazes. You know how to make the bowl. The real challenge becomes how to express a message to the future user of that bowl.

Here's my advice to you at this stage: Move out of your comfort zone. Promote an unsettled atmosphere in your own work. This book is the first step toward experimenting with glazes, clay body formulas, and getting "unstuck." You'll learn troubleshooting techniques and information about clay body formulas and glazes that will empower you to control the results of your work. We'll discuss where clay comes from and why this matters to you, the studio or hobby potter, in the first place. (Quite simply, it goes back to the old input-output theory. You must start with quality materials that fit your application.)

A solid ceramics education should contain many sources of information. As you read and progress in the craft, observe a lot—practice a lot. Find your own voice with the clay. Balance your studio time with classroom or workshop participation. Take advantage of every learning opportunity possible.

A pottery exhibit. Foreground: Chuck Stern. Background: Hiroshi Nakayama

1

Setting Up Shop

FOLLOW THE CLAY: A SENSIBLE WORKING STUDIO

Because creating handmade pottery is labor-intensive, your first priority is to set up an efficient studio layout. Evaluate the layout of your studio with the goal of eliminating wasted motion, increasing floor space, reducing clutter, and creating greater flexibility in production areas. It is only natural to become conditioned by habit to work "around"

problem areas in the studio. At a certain point, accommodating extra bags of clay or glaze materials lying in work areas slows down production and wastes time.

The forming, glazing, firing, and eventual packaging of pottery should follow a step-by-step process, with the studio layout aiding you in reducing inefficiencies and wasted movement. Repeating your efforts or retracing your footsteps in the studio is unproductive.

With fresh eyes, examine the workplace and make a list of items that hinder your ability to make pots. Approach studio layout with this mantra in mind: *Follow the clay.*

Following the clay simply means thinking of how the moist clay will physically move through the studio in every forming, trimming, bisque firing, glazing, glaze firing, and packaging stage. Design a systematic and logical progression of raw materials being turned into pottery or ceramic sculpture. For instance, when throwing clay on the potter's wheel, storage shelves for the pots should be within easy reach. Place all of your trim tools, ribs, sponges, and water buckets within easy reach when you're throwing on the wheel. Construct large sculptural pieces on tables with wheels so you can easily move them about the studio.

Bone-dry pots should be handled with care because they break easily. At this stage the pottery can be slaked down and remixed to form a plastic mass.

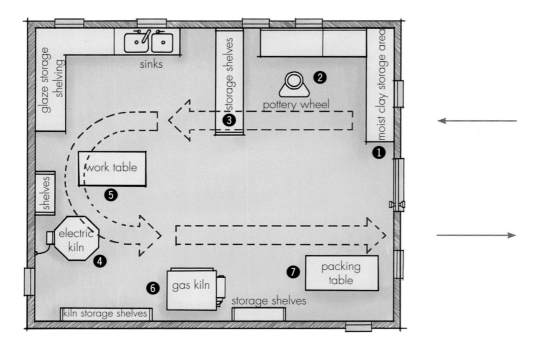

① The moist clay is delivered through the studio door and stored nearby. ② Clay is then moved to the wedging table and forming areas (wheel, hand building), which are adjacent to ③ storage shelving. ④ The pottery is bisque fired in the electric or gas kiln and ⑤ glazed on the work table. After the glazing operation, which may include a spray booth (not shown), pottery moves to the ⑥ kiln for glaze firing and then onto the ⑦ packing table. If the studio is large enough, the packaged pottery can be stored in the studio.

Mapping Studio Movement

The ideal studio setup should enable materials to proceed from one point to another in the production process, uninterrupted. With the illustration above for reference, review the following process.

Clay Storage ①

Whether you mix your own clay or have premixed clay delivered to the studio, it should be readily available for the next step in the production process. Locate your clay delivery areas near your clay storage areas. For dry clay storage, purchase storage bins from ceramic supply companies, or make them yourself with woodshop tools. Ideally, they should be placed under the glaze weigh-out table. Each bin can hold a 50-pound (22.7-kilogram) bag of raw material. Keep a short distance between the bulk storage of materials and weighing-out materials for glaze batches to reduce the time spent moving raw materials. This also decreases the possibility of spilling dry powders that can become airborne.

Work Tables ②

Locate your wedging table and clay forming areas close to moist clay storage. A clay forming area consists of hand building tables and pottery wheels. Keep in mind, moist clay is heavy. One-and-a-half cubic feet of clay weighs 50 pounds (22.7 kg). When clay is moved around the studio without regard to efficient use of labor, you have less time for making pots.

Shelving ③

Flexibility is important for studio shelving design so that tools, supplies, and pottery of different sizes can be stored on the shelves.

Once the moist clay is formed, it can be moved to nearby shelving, where it eventually can be trimmed. Whenever possible, studio-shelf storage areas, worktables, kiln placement, and work areas should reflect the type and scale of pots being produced. For example, 4-inch (10-cm) tall coffee mugs do not require shelves that are 18 inches (46 cm) high.

Bisque Firing Kiln ④

Bone-dry pots are placed into the bisque firing kiln. The size of a kiln, whether it is fired by gas, electricity, or wood, can play an important part in the studio workflow. Although there is no specific rule, several considerations will help determine kiln size. If the kiln is too large, it will take an inordinately long time to fill, delaying the production of finished pottery. If the kiln is too small, it can be excessively labor-intensive loading and unloading the kiln in short intervals.

There is no single kiln size requirement, but many potters use a 7-cubic-foot (approximately 23 3/8 inches [59.4 cm] in diameter by 27 inches [68.6 cm] deep) or a 10-cubic-foot (approximately 28 1/8 inches [71.4 cm] in diameter by 27 inches [68.6 cm] deep) electric kiln, which can bisque or glaze fire pottery. Average-size functional pots, such as cups, plates, pitchers, covered jars, and casseroles can readily fit into kilns of this size. Electric kilns can be purchased in multiple units and added into the production cycle when needed. When possible, with the use of more than one kiln, loading can take place while the other is firing. When using the same size kilns, one bisque firing will yield enough functional pottery to fill 1 1/2 glaze kilns. This is because pots in the bisque kiln can be stacked together, allowing for a larger load of pots per firing. For more information on choosing a kiln, see "What Size Kiln Do You Need?" on page 15.

Glazing Area ⑤ ⑥

After bisque firing, pots can be glazed at a work table or by using a spray booth.

Whenever possible, ease the burden of lifting heavy supplies by adding wheels. For instance, the glaze bucket on wheels pictured on page 15 was constructed by cutting a plywood disk and screwing heavy-duty casters to the bottom of the disk. Remember, glaze containers should be clearly labeled with the glaze name and, when necessary, the firing cone. Label both the body of the bucket and the lid to prevent wasting time locating the correct glaze.

Packing and Storage ⑦

After the pots are removed from the kiln, they can be packaged and sent to a storage area. During this entire process, consider using worktables on wheels, which will allow you to roll ceramic forms around the studio to their eventual completion. Potters constructing large forms should build movable worktables to the same height as their kiln floors. That way, pieces can be slid horizontally into the kiln, reducing labor and preventing breakage.

TIP

Shelving

Kiln shelves are heavy and cumbersome to lift into the kiln. Many potters place kiln shelves on the studio floor. However, designing storage shelves at the same height as the kiln will reduce the amount of bending and lifting taking place when loading shelves into the kiln.

Plan shelving that suits the size and shape of your finished wares.

Pottery pieces in the glaze kiln should be placed close together but not touching; this maximizes space and creates greater thermal mass within the kiln, which will radiate heat during and after the firing.

What Size Kiln Do You Need?

To determine the most efficient kiln size, calculate the amount of pottery you make in a single work cycle. Then figure out how much three-dimensional space your work will fill. Many potters will actually make pottery for a one- or two-week cycle and then stack the unfired pots on shelving to determine how much three-dimensional space the pots will fill. The three-dimensional space required to hold the pots then becomes the cubic feet needed for a kiln.

Studio Economics

Evaluate studio labor costs by asking key questions. First, how expensive will an efficient studio setup be, and will it increase pottery production? Second, will an investment pay for itself in a relatively short period of time?

Weigh the cost of buying an expensive piece of equipment against its increased efficiency. It is sometimes safer to purchase studio furniture where the costs of the items are not that great, so you can earn back your investment in a shorter period of time. For example, if the studio needs extra shelving and worktables, will the expense of buying or constructing studio furniture allow you to produce and store more pottery? Extra space also means you can throw a greater number of cups and place them on nearby shelving.

Evaluate equipment purchases in terms of cost versus benefit. Will the price of a clay extruder, which can mass-produce coils for handles, save time compared to pulling handles from blanks of clay? Cutting costs can be further calculated by asking this question: Can you make more pots per hour because of the investment of equipment versus hands-on forming techniques? At some point in this calculation, you will have to make an aesthetic and philosophical decision on when the handmade process stops and the machine takes over.

Casters alleviate the chore of moving heavy glaze buckets around the studio.

A Studio Suited to Your Needs

The question of studio size depends on your resources and requirements for producing ceramic objects. An average indication of studio size in relation to equipment placement will serve as a starting point for calculating what can be expected from a given square footage. On average, 700 to 800 square feet (65 to 74.3 m²) of studio space can comfortably contain the following:

- a 3′ x 5′ (.9 x 1.5 m) worktable
- a wedging board
- two wheels
- an electric kiln, 7-cubic-foot (198.2 L)
- 4 ware carts 3′ x 4′ x 6′ (.9 x 1.2 x 1.8 m) high
- a deep sink
- one or two tables 8′ x 12′ (2.43 m x 3.65 m)
- a spray booth
- 3 units of shelving 15′ x 2′ (4.6 m x 61 cm) each
- storage space for 2 tons (1,814 kg) of moist clay

The space will give the potter room to walk around pieces of equipment and achieve any wheel throwing or hand building operation. Glazes can be sprayed, brushed, or dipped by the use of the spray booth, or pots can be glazed and placed on any of the worktables. The electric kiln can be used for bisque or glaze firings.

Studio Layout Exercise: Creating a Scale Model

Anticipate potential space and studio layout conflicts by creating a scale model floor plan. It is much easier to move a few pieces of paper around than relocating tons of clay stored too far away from a potter's wheel or forming table. Why move heavy bulky clay around the studio when its strategic placement will result in less labor? Here's how to create a scale model of your studio.

Equipment

- Paper
- Ruler
- Scissors

Instructions

1. Create a paper floor plan of your studio, using a 1″ (2.5 cm) to 1′ (30.5 cm) scale.
2. Record dimensions of kilns, work tables, pug mills, clay mixers, spray booths, and any other studio variables being considered. (Contact the manufacturers for precise dimensions.)
3. Create paper cut-outs of each of your studio variables, using the same 1″ (2.5 cm) to 1′ (30.5 cm) scale.
4. Move the cutouts around your paper floor plan to determine the best arrangement that will accommodate your workflow.

Studio Utilities

A pottery studio needs adequate sources of ventilation, lighting/electric, and water and a reliable heating and cooling system. Think of the studio as your home away from home, where you will spend a great deal of time and effort. Cave in to creature comforts such as heating or air conditioning, which will make your studio more comfortable throughout the seasons and contribute to production efficiency.

Safety is always a concern. A clean studio is a safe studio, so invest in a studio vacuum and mop. Secure hoses and electrical cords so they do not become obstacles. And seriously evaluate the following three studio necessities: ventilation, lighting/electric, and water.

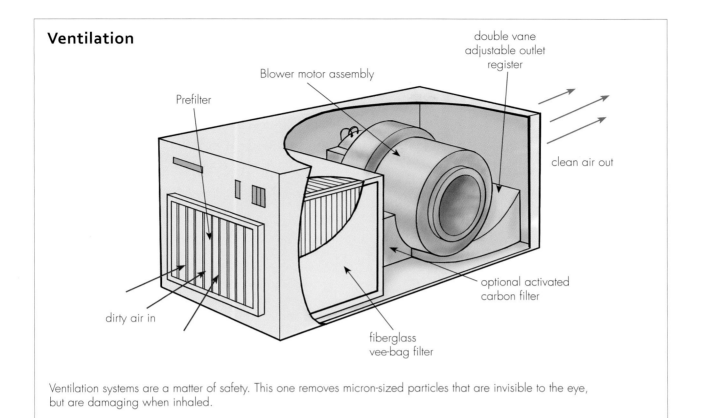

Ventilation

Prefilter

Blower motor assembly

double vane adjustable outlet register

clean air out

dirty air in

optional activated carbon filter

fiberglass vee-bag filter

Ventilation systems are a matter of safety. This one removes micron-sized particles that are invisible to the eye, but are damaging when inhaled.

Ventilation

In venting the studio space, there are two primary concerns: the steady flow of clean air through the studio and appropriate venting of kilns and equipment contained in the studio. The clay dust particles you can see are not the problem. The micron-size particles you can't see could enter the lungs, causing respiratory distress or more serious illnesses.

Any studio venting system should capture micron-size particles in a filtering unit. Many companies offer whole room air-filtering systems that can be installed in any studio.

Specific studio equipment, such as grinding wheels, pug mills, and clay mixers, should have individual venting systems to remove solid particles thrown into the air. Gas and electric kilns must have their own venting systems to remove the products of combustion.

As a complement to your venting systems, it's important to keep the walls of the studio free of any items or surfaces that will catch dust, such as pictures or any decorative displays. If possible, remove molding or trim from walls.

Lighting and Electrical

Proper lighting will reduce your eyestrain and fatigue. Place pottery wheels, glazing areas, and worktables near natural sources of lighting. Also, incorporate adequate lighting near kilns and full-spectrum florescent lighting above work areas. Also helpful are low-voltage halogen fixtures directed at specific zones in the studio.

Keep in mind, the choice of studio wall color will enhance both artificial and natural light. White—or at least light-colored—walls will reflect any available light source, accentuating the equipment and finished wares.

Electric requirements for the studio are most important for power tools, potter's wheels, lighting, heating, kilns, and other appliances. Inadequate electrical capacity can slow production. Most new construction supplies nearly twice as much amperage service to buildings as what is delivered to old, residential buildings. Remember, a small kiln (such as 7-cubic-foot [198 L] or 10-cubic-foot [283.2 L]) can usurp nearly half of a residential building's electrical supply. Many industrial buildings have three-phase capacity, and kilns for this type of electrical supply have to be special ordered from the factory.

The Retail Studio

A pottery studio located in a commercial district can attract walk-in customer traffic. While you'll pay higher rent for a space in a high-traffic area, the extra expense can pay off in product sales when passersby are intrigued by beautiful window displays filled with your finished work. Potential customers who are interested in handmade objects are naturally drawn to viewing the process. A studio/retail combination gives the public a chance to watch the potter at work, which is always a crowd pleaser. A display area within or adjacent to the studio exhibiting the finished ware also can help generate sales.

Retail tip: Don't forget to develop a mailing list of your customers. Send them an invitation before a kiln is due to be opened. This gives an interested population the opportunity to view and purchase pots warm from the kiln.

A window display with attractive pottery lures passersby into this working gallery.

Before moving into a new studio or remodeling a studio space, always be sure there is more than adequate electrical supply for all lighting and appliances. Electricians familiar with kiln operations and kiln manufacturers are good sources of information on meeting the electrical capacity for the studio.

Water

Having a source of clean hot and cold water in the studio is a critical resource for any pottery producing operation. Water is used in mixing glazes, clay-forming operations, and in studio cleanup procedures. A water source within the studio is also an important safety factor because any time water has to be carried in from outside of the studio, there is always the possibility of spillage and creating a slippery floor. If that water mixes with any clay left on the studio floor, it can create an especially slick, unsafe surface.

A deep sink with a gooseneck hose will allow you to clean glaze buckets and tools quickly and efficiently. If possible, the sink should be located near glaze mixing areas and centrally located in your studio. Try to avoid a situation in which a sink is located on another level from the studio area. Constantly walking up and down stairs to obtain water is labor-intensive, time consuming, and possibly hazardous.

Because sink wastewater will contain a percentage of solid particles from glaze materials and clay, research the correct drain installation traps, so pipes and leach fields or sewer systems do not become clogged with solids. You can make a catch trap yourself or buy one. Several commercial catch traps fit under sinks, allowing the solids to accumulate in a container and the liquids to proceed down the drain and out of the studio. Whether you make a catch trap yourself or buy one, clean out the solids container.

Task lighting illuminates this pottery. Notice that a wide variety of glaze colors and surface textures are easily apparent. A well-lighted studio is important to view work. Good lighting also reduces eye strain and promotes an efficient production cycle.

A POTTER'S TOOL CHEST

Making pottery is a labor-intensive activity involving many steps that require repetitive motion: wedging and rolling out slabs of clay, throwing forms on the potter's wheel, and trimming pots. These procedures introduce the potential for hand or back injury. Any steps you take to reduce fatigue and injury translate into increased productivity and profit—and, at the very least, greater comfort while you work.

A potter's essentials

A potter's essentials:

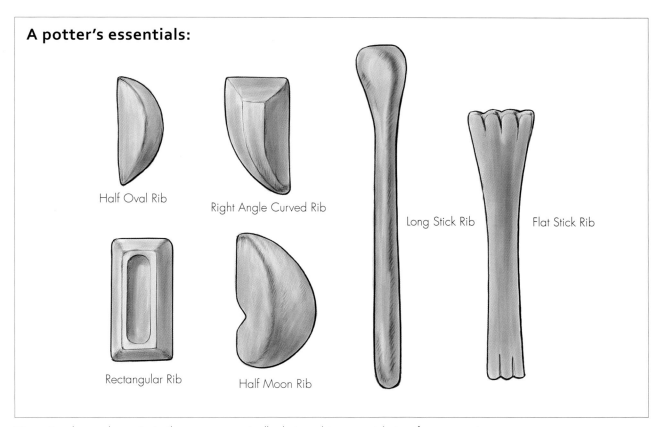

Half Oval Rib

Right Angle Curved Rib

Long Stick Rib

Flat Stick Rib

Rectangular Rib

Half Moon Rib

Dimensional, wooden potter's ribs are ergonomically designed to accurately transfer pressure to the moist clay surface. Each rib is fabricated from close-grained hardwood and is sculpted to comfortably fit the hand.

Did You Know...

The National Council on Education for the Ceramic Arts sponsored a survey of U.S. potters in 2000. One of the four highest-rated health issues reported at every level of experience was hand injury.

Ergonomic Pottery Tools

Ergonomic tools will help protect your hands and reduce stress from direct, repeated contact with clay. Choose tools that are functional, comfortable, and reduce strain on the hands. Poorly designed tools will create uncomfortable pressure points on the fingers, which will be compounded by the repetitive actions of shaping and trimming pots.

The repetitive use of tools, or any motion by the hand, can result in muscle strain or ligament damage. In worst-case scenarios, prolonged repetitive movement can cause carpal tunnel syndrome, which is an inflammation of the median nerve that runs through the carpal tunnel bones and ligaments in the wrist. Carpal tunnel syndrome causes pain and pressure with a tingling sensation in the wrists or forearms. The best preventive step is to choose ergonomic tools.

Rib Tools

A rib tool is an extension of the potter's hand. The rib tool serves multiple functions when brought into contact with pliable clay. It can impart straight or curved profiles, altering the clay's surface, or it can be used to burnish or smooth those surfaces. Wooden, plastic, rubber, and metal ribs of diverse profiles and sizes are readily available. You can purchase them at ceramics supply stores.

Because ribs are used so often, they should be comfortable. Wooden ribs are softer on the hand than metal ones, and they float in the water bucket used in the clay-forming process, making the ribs easier to retrieve. A precisely designed, dimensional rib offers increased flexibility and control during repetitive forming operations. Additionally, the significant weight and balance of this tool enables easy manipulation of clay surfaces during hand-building or wheel-throwing procedures. The many uses for a rib are limited only by your imagination. Following are photographs of some helpful ribs.

① Right Angle Curved Rib

② Rectangular Rib

③ Half Oval Rib

④ Long Stick Rib

⑤ Flat Stick Rib

① **The Right Angle Curved Rib** has three planes that can impart a straight edge or curved surface to clay.

② **The Rectangular Rib** is designed for flat areas with an easy grip indented interior section.

③ **The Half Oval Rib** imparts a curved or flat surface to clay. The small size allows for placement in recessed areas.

④ **The Long Stick Rib** can be used to form interior curves inside narrow-necked shapes. Each end of the rib has a different curved surface.

⑤ **The Flat Stick Rib** has a grooved surface that can be used to impress parallel concave lines in most clay.

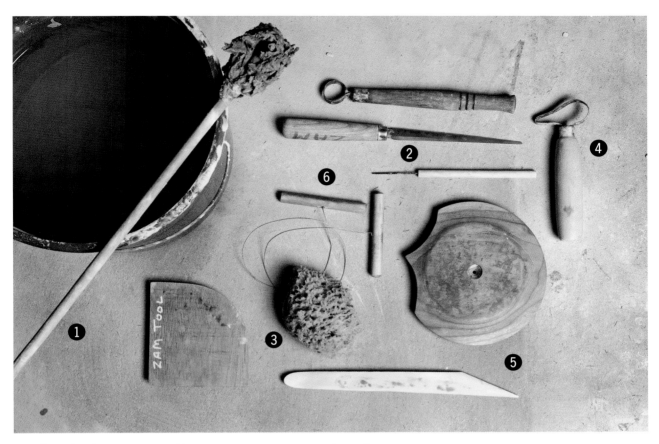

Needle tools, ribs, sponges, and knives are common pottery tools used to shape and manipulate ceramic surfaces.

① **Sponge on a stick** can be a homemade tool prepared by tying a sponge onto a dowel with dental floss. Its purpose is to wick away water from the bottom of thrown forms.

② **Needle tools** are used to cut off excess clay on the wheel and for roughing up clay surfaces for aesthetic purposes or to join two pieces (such as a handle on a coffee mug).

③ **Sponges** come in handy for removing excess water from the pottery during the throwing process or for adding water to the piece. A sponge is also necessary for cleanup. Choose small sponges for throwing (or cut up a larger sponge) and large block-shaped sponges for cleaning work surfaces, such as a canvas-covered forming table.

④ **Metal trim tools** are used when a piece is leather hard. During the trimming process, before the work is fired in the kiln, a potter will return the pot to the wheel and use a metal trim tool to form a "foot" for a pot or simply shave away clay to create a smooth, even surface.

⑤ **Wooden forming tools** can be used to score or shape moist clay.

⑥ **Wire cut off tools** can be used to section off moist clay.

2

The Nature of Clay

WHAT IS CLAY?

Clay is a more complex amalgamation of ingredients than you might realize. Moist clay, whether you prepare it or purchase it from a ceramics supply company, can contain various mixtures of clay(s), flint, feldspar, talc, grog, and other ceramic raw materials. The individual raw materials are combined in different amounts and ratios to form a clay body formula.

The clay body's fired color can be white, tan, brown, or any color with the additions of metallic coloring oxides or stains. Each forming method, firing range, color, or firing technique will determine the amount and type of specific ceramic materials that will be used in the clay body. If the clay body formula is developed correctly, the best qualities of each raw material will ensure quality finished pottery.

An **earthenware clay body** (generally fired below 1,945°F [1,063°C]) is a low-temperature clay, which in the raw state can be white, brown, red, gray, or black, depending on its organic and mineral content. When fired, it is porous and commonly used for flowerpots.

A **stoneware clay body** designates a high-temperature clay (2,232°F [1,222°C] or higher), which is dense, hard, and vitreous when fired.

A **porcelain clay body** designates a high-temperature, vitreous, white clay body (2,232°F [1,222°C]) that can be translucent when thin.

A **raku clay body** is designed to be fast-fired at a low temperature (approximately 1,828°F [998°C]), taken out of the kiln, and fast-cooled. Raku can be glazed or unglazed and placed in an oxidation or reduction atmosphere to achieve various clay body and glaze colors.

A **salt/soda clay body** is formulated to accept a sodium vapor glaze by introducing salt or soda ash during the kiln firing. The vapor produced interacts with the body surface, forming a distinctive "orange peel" glaze of sodium, alumina, and silicate.

Note: Raw clay color often does not represent its eventual fired color. Variations can be caused by the chemical composition of the clay, its organic content, the kiln atmosphere it is fired in, and the temperature it is taken to in the kiln.

Previous page: The color of raw clay can change once it is fired due its organic content and chemical composition. Many clays appear black or gray in their raw state but are white once fired.

Shrapnel Effect

Mechanical water is removed in the bisque heating cycle by 212° F (100°C). If the clay is heated too fast in the first stages of bisque firing, mechanical water turns to steam, which expands and will cause the pot to crack or, in extreme cases, blow up. This is commonly known as the **shrapnel effect**, and it can also induce adjoining pots to crack or blow up. That's why it is always best to fire the bisque kiln slowly, allowing the protracted safe release of steam.

Clay Components

The central component of any clay body is clay, which can be a diverse hydro alumina silicate platelet structure material, depending on the type of clay or clays used. Clay is unique in that no other material has so many individual qualities of structural bonding on different levels, resulting in plasticity and fired strength. In other aspects, clay is ordinary because it is found on every continent on Earth and under its oceans. One theory states that the size and layered shape of clay platelets were the perfect platform for the growth of amino acids, the building blocks of eventual life on Earth.

Every type of clay is unique, but there are some similar components, which we'll talk about in turn: mechanical water, chemical water, organic content, pH levels, particle size, mineral content, loss on ignition, tramp materials, and crude color.

Mechanical Water

Mechanical water in clay is the moisture content that makes clay feel plastic. It is also the atmospheric moisture that the clay takes on in the studio. (In contrast, the chemical water is contained in any raw material that contains chemical water, such as clay, which is 1 Al_2O_3 2 SiO_2 2 H_2O.) The amount of water added for plasticity depends on the specific clay body formula. Clay bodies for Ram pressing, which is ware formed in a plaster mold by injecting air into the mold and releasing the form, will require less water than throwing clay bodies, because the greater forces of the hydraulic press can shape the clay more efficiently with less water. Also, ball clays and bentonites have greater surface areas that require more water for plasticity.

Generally speaking, mechanical water content makes up 18 to 22 percent of a clay body formula. Bagged dry clay moisture content averages 1 to 4 percent. When a ceramics supplier or individual potter mixes clay, more water is added to obtain a plastic workable mass, and the clay's moisture content increases to 25 to 28 percent, which is suitable for various types of forming operations. It is important to note that the water source can alter the forming properties of the moist clay. Water containing high levels of calcium will cause flocculation (knitting together of the moist clay), while high levels of sodium will cause deflocculation (soft, wobbly moist clay) properties in moist clay.

Once the moist clay is taken out of its plastic bag, it begins to stiffen, due to water loss. There are various stages of mechanical water loss. The **leather-hard** stage is when clay is cold and damp to the touch and non-plastic. **Bone-dry** clay changes to a lighter color, and all visible water is absent. Bone-dry clay is brittle and not plastic. At this stage, the clay is at its most fragile and can easily be broken. A common misconception is that if we let the bone-dry clay further dry for months or years in our studios, it will become drier. Unfortunately, at some point the clay assumes the moisture content of the studio, which means there is still mechanical water trapped within the so-called dry clay.

This cracked pot is the result of a kiln heating or cooling too quickly.

One type of blister in the glaze is formed when carbonaceous material in the clay body is not completely driven off during the first stages of the bisque firing. The carbonaceous material remaining in the clay body then turns into a gas, which is released into the glaze during the subsequent glaze firing.

Chemical Water

Chemical water is part of the hidden structure contained within the clay body. Clay is theoretically composed of 1 part alumina, 2 parts silica, and 2 parts chemical water, which can be stated as Al_2O_3 2 SiO_2 2 H_2O. During the bisque firing process, if the chemical water component of clay is released too quickly, pots can crack in the first stages of the bisque firing. Also keep in mind, once chemical water is removed, the clay can never be rehydrated to form a plastic mass.

Organic Content

Clays contain organic material from the breakdown of plant life, twigs, and roots during the clay's formation process in the earth. Each clay type contains a different level of organic material, which can fluctuate from one part of a clay deposit to the next. Furthermore, organic material can burn out of the clay at different temperatures during the

firing. During firing, carbon released from organic content can turn into gas at higher temperatures and cause pinholes and blisters in glaze surfaces, or bloating in the clay body. A long-duration, clean (oxidation atmosphere) bisque firing to 1,200°F (649°C) will completely remove any carbon from organic content.

pH Levels

Alkalinity or acidity of clay is referred to as pH level. Most clays are slightly acidic (4.5 to 6.5). Neutral is 7.0, and higher than 7.0 is alkaline. The pH level can vary as much as 0.5 within the same batch of clay. Acidic clays and raw materials cause moist clay bodies to bind together, resulting in greater plasticity and improved forming characteristics. When throwing on the wheel, moist clay will stand up more firmly between pulls. In throwing and hand building, a clay body's flocculation caused by acidic conditions in the

Organic material that has not been completely removed from clay during early firing stages becomes carbon, which combines with iron and silica into powerful flux, causing deformation.

If excess oxygen in not present in the first stages of the bisque firing, organic material in the clay is trapped, which can cause bloating in the fired clay. If the clay body contains iron and there is a lack of oxygen in the kiln, carbon monoxide is formed with carbon present in the clay to produce black coring, as shown above left.

moist state is a beneficial quality. The moist clay "knits" together and does not deform under pressure.

The opposite effect occurs when alkaline clay or raw materials are present in a clay body. Alkaline materials promote thixotropy, a condition that causes moist clay to soften under pressure. A clay body with a high pH alkaline level is rubbery and sticky when thrown on the wheel or used in hand building. After pulling up a form on the wheel, you'll notice slurry clay on your hands. That is because alkaline clay bodies cause clay particles to repel each other, resulting in minimal clay adhesion. Poor handling qualities of high alkaline raw materials are most noticeable in porcelain clay bodies. Soluble alkalis can cause thixotropy in stoneware, Raku, salt/soda (sodium carbonate vapor firing), and earthenware. In slip casting clay bodies, a variation in pH levels (acidity/alkalinity) from the water source or raw materials can affect the deflocculation requirements for each batch of slip, causing changes in viscosity.

Particle Size

Clays are composed of very small platelet structures that interact with water on many levels to form a plastic mass. While all dry clay looks like fine powder, there can be quite a difference in the sizes of platelets contained within that powder. Clay platelet size and the distribution of sizes depend on the type of clay. For instance, fireclays have a larger platelet size than ball clays.

Particle-size distribution within a specific type of clay (i.e. ball clays, fireclay, earthenware clay, stoneware clays, and bentonites) can be critical in determining the clay's handling qualities. Particle-size distribution reflects the range of platelet sizes in a particular clay. For example, if there are too many small platelets in a clay, excessive warping and shrinkage can occur. A high percentage of small platelets will have a greater surface area, requiring more water to achieve plasticity. In such a case, moist clay can have a gummy or rubber-like feel in forming operations. Drying cracks can develop where a handle or other piece of clay meets the body of the pot. This type of crack is caused when water evaporates from the pot, leaving dry clay platelets hanging in mid air.

Even the best, quality-controlled raw materials are sometimes inconsistent in terms of particle size, chemical composition, and organic content. What happens when particle size is inconsistent? Let's take fireclay as an

Diagram of Clay Particles and Water in Suspension

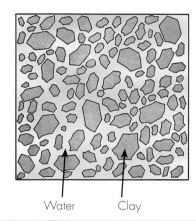

The hexagonal clay plates feature a 10:1 ratio of length to thickness. Average particle sizes are 100 microns to 0.1 microns.

Water   Clay

example, because it is noted for its inconsistency. Fireclays can constitute 15 to 30 percent of the clay component in many stoneware clay body formulas and, by definition, are coarse and refractory. Occasionally, these clays can contain large nodules (2 to 3 mm) of manganese dioxide and iron. Large nodules of manganese in clay can produce black spit-outs, or depressions in the fired clay's surface caused by the decomposition of gas when manganese is heated. Iron oxide particles tend to produce brown, smooth, irregular-shaped blotches on the clay's surface. Both conditions are visible when fireclays are fired in reduction kiln atmospheres.

TIP

Clay Texture

Clay and water together form a dynamic system that behaves differently in various storage conditions. For example, a moist clay body can slowly depart from a flocculated (tight) to partially deflocculated (rubbery) state over a period of time in storage, due to the breakdown of alkaline materials within the clay body. While not generally considered as a variable in moist clay production, the pH level of the water used to mix the clay can alter handling and forming qualities by increasing the release of soluble alkaline materials in the clay body.

Soluble salts can migrate to the clay body surface during the drying stage.

Mineral Content

The mineral content of any clay can change radically depending on the type of clay. For example, ball clays typically contain 75 percent kaolinite, 20 percent free silica, and 5 percent trace elements.

However, free silica, which is the silica not bound up with the clay particle, in ball clay can average from 15 to 30 percent. Free silica exists in the form of silica crystals floating around the clay particles. Free silica goes through quartz inversion at 1,063°F (573°C) upon heating and cooling in the kiln. During the 2,012° to 2,282°F (1,100° to 1,250°C) range, silica in the clay changes to cristobalite, which goes through an inversion upon cooling in the 392°F (200°C) in the cooling cycle. High levels of silica in the clay body in any form can cause heating and cooling cracks. Free silica is also very refractory, which can increase the maturing range of a clay body, causing glaze problems and high absorption rates in the fired clay body.

Loss on Ignition

Loss on ignition (L.O.I.) is the loss in weight of a clay when it is heated under specific conditions. L.O.I. is stated as a percentage of the clay's dry weight. In ball clays, chemical water is the largest component in L.O.I., followed by organic materials, which are carbon. Any sulphate found in the clay is the smallest part of the total percentage in the L.O.I. component.

Ceramic raw materials are usually white, off-white, tan, brown, or various shades in between. The organic content and naturally occuring metallic oxides, such as iron, manganese, and rutile can alter the raw material color. Frequently, they do not look like their raw color when fired.

Tramp Materials

As the name implies, tramp materials can hitch a ride with clays and the raw materials commonly found in clay bodies or glazes. They're also known as contaminants. In some instances, tramp materials cause defects, but they can also enhance the aesthetic or functional quality of a fired ceramic piece. Contamination found in clays can range from coal, lignite, and other organic materials to, surprisingly, metal nuts, bolts, and cigarettes. This last category of contamination speaks more to poor quality control and packaging at the mine.

It is possible to formulate a clay body or glaze based on pure oxides of silica, alumina, iron, calcium, magnesium, potassium, and sodium. However, the clay will not exhibit the same handling or fired qualities as the mined raw material containing the identical percentages of the pure oxides. That's because the occurrence of tramp and/or organic material associated with clays often increases their plasticity and handling characteristics, along with contributing visual uniqueness that would not be evident in clays that are theoretically "pure."

Still, there are limitations as to the type, size, shape, and amount of tramp material that can be present in a clay before it will cause problems. These limitations are based on functional considerations and personal aesthetic goals. For example, relatively large nodules of feldspar (1/8 inch [3 mm] in diameter) found in some types of clay can cause raised bumps of fused, white spots on a fired clay body surface. Although these irregular areas might look pleasing on sculptural pieces, the same nodules on the rim of a coffee mug will be less than pleasant.

Clay deposits found in natural settings, such as this one, can contain metallic oxides and organic material. Contaminates found within the clay itself, along with processing and transportation debris, can be found in raw materials. In some instances, they go unnoticed and do not alter the fired clay body. Occasionally, they are the cause of clay body and glaze defects.

Crude Color

Each clay blend has a characteristic crude color, whether it is tan, off-white, white, buff, or brown. Crude color does not always indicate the fired color of a clay. For example, crude color comes from carbon in some clays, but some very dark crude color clays with low carbon fire-out white.

If you receive a new batch of clay that is a completely different crude color than you expected, the cause may be as simple as a shipping mistake or clay-mixing mistake. Any time a raw material is re-bagged, there is the possibility of error. To avoid this problem, buy full bags (50 or 100 pounds [22.7 or 45.4 kg]) of clay and raw materials. Also, be sure to test every batch of clay or raw material before committing it to full production.

The Origin of Clay

Clay is formed by a series of geological events that break down rock formed by volcanic action. The deposit can remain on-site as primary clay, which is white in color, with large particle sizes lacking in plastic qualities. Secondary clays are transported by wind and water action and can accumulate impurities before settling into a sediment layer. Secondary clays are darker in fired color, and they have smaller particle sizes, causing greater plasticity than primary clays.

At some point in the primary or secondary transformation process, clays are mined from the ground. There are many individual clays within the primary and secondary clay categories. There are wide ranges of particle size, chemical composition, organic content, and contamination that can fluctuate over short or long periods of time. Considering that inconsistencies are always present in any one batch of clay, it is remarkable that clay body failures do not occur with greater frequency.

Clay Mining Operations

In a typical clay mining operation, test holes are drilled in a geologically likely place, which will indicate the estimated reserves of a particular type of clay deposit. A specific block or area of clay is defined, and the overburden or topsoil is removed, exposing the underlying seams of clay. In some deposits, the overburden can be screened to remove sand or gravel, which can then be sold to construction and landscape contractors. Most deposits have overburden stockpiled for later use in reclaiming of the mine. (Overburden is the top sand or soil that contains trees, shrubs, and brush, which, after mining operations, is replaced to make the land look like it did before excavation.)

One clay deposit can cover approximately 20 acres (80,937 m²) and produce 4,000,000 tons (3,628,739 metric tons) of clay. Most clay companies mine fewer than 20 end-point clays, which they blend into market-grade clay. Clay mining companies may sell dozens of different blended grades of clay and more than 100 years' reserve, depending on geological conditions at each site. A clay mine's objective is to consistently blend individual clays to ensure uniformity of products for their major market customers.

If you visit a clay mining operation and see how the material is harvested, processed, packaged, and shipped, you'll gain some insight on why clay body inconsistencies exist and just how many "blips" can occur that will affect your finished product.

① After the clay deposits are located, scrapers and tractors remove an overburden consisting of sand, shale, or mineral content.

② The open clay pit is exposed, and different clay seams of clay are excavated.

③ An excavator places clay in a truck. The clay truck goes to a drying area, and then the clay is sent to the grinding operation, where it is reduced in size and eventually separated by particle size.

④ At a screening operation, sand and gravel are separated from the overburden

⑤ Air-floated clay is stored in these silos.

⑥ Clay is packed in 50-pound (22.7 kg) bags and 2,000-pound (907-kg) bulk sacks for shipment.

⑦ The overburden is returned to the site.

Slab Construction Oval Platter, by Jim Fineman, 1" (2.5 cm) tall, 10¹/₂" (26 cm) diameter
Firing: cone 9 (2,300°F [1,260°C]), reduction atmosphere
See page 157 for formula

Dynamic Clay

The one constant when working with any raw material
is ongoing change or alteration. The actual raw materials
that comprise clay bodies are always shifting in mechanical
water content, chemical water content, organic content,
pH level, particle size, mineral content, and tramp material. Several factors can alter a clay body. Some of these
factors take place subtly over years, but others are more
dramatic, occurring immediately after the first bag of clay
is opened.

Changing clay can affect a finished product's color and
glaze fit. For example, higher iron content in a clay can
result in a darker fired color. Or a shift in a clay's silica content, which changes the rate at which a clay body shrinks
or expands, can adversely influence glaze fit. Sometimes
a change will occur in a single bag of clay, causing clay or
glaze defects. Occasionally, a clay alters over a period of
months or years, causing a slow transformation in a clay
body color or texture. While mines and ceramics suppliers strive for consistency—and for the most part they

succeed—a few small changes in clays can add up to a big
change for the entire clay body formula. Unfortunately,
clay variations are mostly reflected in the finished ware.

If you choose to mix your own clay body formula, as
opposed to ordering clay from a supplier, you will have
more immediate control over the weighing and mixing
process. But direct control does not always translate into
improved quality. Even when mixing one's own clay, a
defective clay component in the formula is often discov-
ered only when the finished ware is removed from the kiln.
There are many reasons for a clay body to fluctuate, some
of which involve a predetermined adjustment by potters
who mix their own clay or the ceramics supplier who mixes
and sells moist clay. A clay body can also fluctuate, due to
inaccurately weighing the dry materials or incorrect mixing procedures. Knowledge and expertise in mixing clay
can prevent these problems. You will decide whether it is
appropriate and efficient for you to mix clay yourself or to
purchase it from a supplier.

ACQUIRING CLAY: BUY PREMIXED OR MIX YOUR OWN?

All potters wrestle with what is the best method of ensuring a good supply of moist clay. As beginning students, we were supplied with premixed clay at school, camp, or craft centers. Our main concern was mastering the skills needed to form pottery or sculpture. Clay was clay, as long as you could mold, shape, and work it into a finished product. But years later in your ceramics education, you may ask yourself: Should I mix my own clay or buy it premixed from a supplier?

Potters bounce back and forth on the clay supply issue. A defective shipment of clay might inspire you to try your hand at mixing your own. Or, the labor-intensive experience of doing just that may cause you to seek a reliable supplier who can do the work while you concentrate on producing pottery to sell or show. There are pros and cons to mixing your own and to ordering premixed moist clay from a ceramics supplier. Mixing clay is labor-intensive and requires time, tools, and practiced technique—not to mention the appropriate clay body. There is no cheating. On the other hand, just because you purchase premixed moist clay from a supplier does not mean the material will be flawless.

What is the best solution to the clay supply question? Only you can decide.

Clay Bodies

The combination of clays, feldspars, talc, grog, and other materials constitute a clay body. Clay bodies include various blends of these raw materials, depending on the temperature range, forming method, shrinkage, absorption, fired color, and function of the finished ceramic object in mind. Some clay body formulas contain only one ingredient; others contain many different clays and raw materials.

Making good pots or sculpture depends on the suitability, accuracy, and consistency of the clay body formula, whether the clay is mixed in the studio or arrives premixed from a ceramics supply company. The first question potters should consider is whether their clay body produces the results they need. If so, the next question is how to obtain a consistent supply.

Left to right: ball clay, talc, kaolin, bentonite, feldspar, and flint are used to create a clay body formula.

Clay Body Components

The success of a clay body formula depends on the reliability of its components. Clay bodies contain several raw materials, which are quality controlled in relation to particle-size distribution, organic content, pH factor, and chemical composition. Many ceramics suppliers will reveal the types of clays used in a clay body, which gives clues to the clay body's dependability. However, suppliers will rarely give the exact amounts of each clay or other material used in the clay body because that is proprietary information. A more accurate indication is the clay's track record with other potters who are using it in similar applications and firing conditions. Here are a few generalities to keep in mind:

- Established materials—such as kaolins, ball clays, talcs, whiting, wollastonite, bentonites, feldspars, and flint—are used in the paint, paper, sanitary ware, glass, and other large industries and are best suited for pottery production.

- Earthenware, stoneware, and fireclays can be more trouble-prone, due to their unrefined nature.

- Fireclays can contain high levels of contamination from manganese and iron nodules, coal, lignite, sand, and other contaminants.

- Some earthenware clays have random deposits of lime, which can cause lime pop, producing a semicircular crack in the bisque or glaze fired ware.

Stock Clay Body Formulas and Custom Formulas

Ceramics supply companies sell stock clay body formulas of different firing ranges, colors, and forming qualities for hand building or throwing. They are usually characterized by stability and consistency of performance. Another category of moist clay consists of custom clay bodies or, as they are called, private formulas. Individual potters develop custom clay bodies, which are mixed either by the potter or by the ceramics supply company. The reliability of the clay body depends in large part on the ability of the ceramics supplier to adhere exactly to the amounts of raw materials specified. In private or custom clay body formulas, the potter's knowledge of ceramic materials is critical in obtaining a good result.

The predominant materials in a clay body formula will indicate how the clay will behave in the forming and firing stages. For example, if a clay body contains high percentages of ball clay, a very plastic clay, it can be smooth in handling operations but shrink excessively during drying and firing. Because of their small platelet size, ball clays require greater amounts of water to achieve plasticity. Upon drying, the clay body can shrink excessively and/or warp.

On the other hand, if a clay body contains high levels of fireclay, a refractory coarse clay, it can be nonplastic and difficult to form on the potter's wheel. Clays with high iron content, such as low-temperature earthenware, Redart and high-temperature stoneware Newman Red, can produce darker clay body colors depending on the percentage used in the clay body formula. With a thorough knowledge of each type of clay used in the clay body formula, you can estimate the clay body's handling and firing characteristics.

Reliable Formulas

When mixing your own clay body, research the reliability of the formula to reduce potential defects. A reliable clay body formula can function with slight variations in raw material, and it can also accept slight variations in kiln atmosphere and firing temperatures. Deviation of 1 or 2 percent in raw materials will not cause a significant difference in the clay body's forming characteristics or fired qualities. The best situation is to produce pottery or sculpture that allows for slight variations in size, texture, and color. Some potters make the mistake of trying to produce items to exact specifications, only to find that their raw materials and forming methods cannot meet such an ideal. Large commercial dinnerware manufacturers invest millions of dollars in forming perfect plates, and, even then, 30 percent of their production can have defects.

Test for Reliability

Whether you mix your own clay or buy it premixed, mark a few pots from each new batch of clay to distinguish each batch as it goes through the production process. If a problem develops, the entire production from the suspect batch can be set aside for further testing. If the pots were not coded, it may be hard to figure out which batch of clay was responsible for the defects.

A ceramics supplier's screening operation will improve clay body quality by eliminating unwanted contaminants.

① **Screen.** An adjustable series of 30 mesh to 150 mesh, 72" (1.8 m) diameter stainless steel screens vibrate to trap oversize clay particles or contaminants from entering the clay batch.

② **Magnet.** Reduces iron specks in white or red clay bodies passing through to the clay hopper.

③ **Clay hopper.** The stainless steel container captures the processed clay, which is then taken to the clay mixer and pug mill.

TIP

Screen Contaminants

Some clay body formulas require fireclays, earthenware, and stoneware clays, but their use must be monitored. Ask your supplier about screening to decrease the amount of contaminants that have accumulated in the mining and processing stages.

Consistency in a clay body allows potters to create sets and series.

Mixing Your Own Clay

Mixing your own clay offers the intangible benefit of being completely involved in the pottery endeavor. Many people first started to realize their artistic goals in ceramics and, for them, the whole activity of mixing clay and making pots or sculpture are intrinsically tied together. Monetary rewards and the breakdown of production costs are not relevant factors in such situations. For potters pursuing a total involvement in all aspects of ceramics, the process is equally as important as the final product.

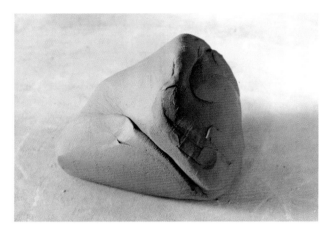

The ability to customize clay bodies lures potters into mixing their own formulas.

One major advantage of mixing your own clay is the greater flexibility in adjusting the clay body formula and moisture content, which gives you overall quality control. However, carefully weigh whether the process is worth the labor, effort, and expense.

Before mixing your own clay, ask yourself: Does the clay body depend on a specific finished color? Do the forming qualities of the moist clay require an exact clay body formula? Does the clay require a specific moisture content? If yes, consider mixing your own clay. For example, clay bodies containing nylon or fiberglass fibers used for structural strength are difficult for ceramics suppliers to mix, due to the time-consuming process of cleaning clay mixers and pug mills. Ceramics suppliers are not set up to mix, such custom formulas, leaving potters to mix it themselves.

Another advantage of mixing your own clay is that, as long as you have the raw materials on hand, you'll have a ready supply of moist clay. You can mix the amount of clay desired and control the supply, which is especially important in a production situation.

A third advantage of mixing your own clay is that you can mix and test a variety of clay bodies and make timely revisions to clay body formulas. However, understand that mixing your own clay will require knowledge of raw materials and the ability to formulate a clay body.

Should You Reprocess Trimmings?

Reprocessing trimmings prevents waste; however, clay is dirt-cheap, and your labor is expensive. Is reprocessing worth the effort? The time and labor required to store and mix clay trimmings might be better used for more profitable projects. Plus, if you mix your own clay, reprocessing scraps also means incurring the same clay mixing time and labor efforts expended the first time the clay was mixed. Remember, more time spent reprocessing clay is less time spent making pots.

Recycling clay allows potters to maximize raw materials, but the process is not always efficient.

Mixing Equipment

Mixing your own clay can be capital intensive: it requires the purchase of clay mixers and pug mills. An added cost is inevitable maintenance and repairs. The money you spend to buy and maintain a clay mixer and pug mill could be spent instead for other purposes that might return a greater profit. If you try to get by buying smaller clay mixers and pug mills, your unintended result could be slower clay production and possibly higher maintenance costs with underpowered, inadequately designed machines. But if you buy larger machines, they'll cost more upfront, and they can result in unused production capacity. That's why it's important to take time to research and find the best machines for your individual production requirements.

Mixed Clay Storage

If you mix your own clay, you'll also need to purchase and store your materials. Plan your dry clay orders so a steady supply is always available, causing no delays in mixing operations. Buying in bulk results in a lower cost per pound of materials, but you also must have the space to store dry clay. Designate areas close to your production space for clay mixing and storage for dry and wet clay. This will save labor and time—and, remember, the more you touch the clay, the more it costs.

Get Equipped to Mix Clay

Simply mixing the dry clay body formula and adding the appropriate amount of water is all that is really required to achieve a plastic mass of usable clay. Traditionally, hand mixing or blending clays and other ceramic raw materials was the only method available to achieve workable consistency clay. Today, hand mixing clay will accomplish the goal, but mixing machines and pug mills will save labor and time when you require greater quantities of uniform-consistency, moist clay.

Whatever method is used, each clay platelet should be surrounded by a film of water with all the other raw materials in the clay body blended into a uniform mass for optimum plasticity.

A pug mill extrudes a compacted cylinder of clay.

These super sacks of dry clay require plenty of storage. While your studio mixing operation won't require these large bags, you still must plan space for raw materials and mixing equipment.

Clay Mixer and Pug Mill

The most efficient and popular way to mix clay is with a clay mixer and pug mill. Ceramics supply companies use both machines in their productions. Specific amounts of dry clay and water are blended in the mixer, and then the moist clay is placed in the pug mill and compressed by a mechanical screw. The compressed clay then goes through a chamber where the air is removed, and then the clay is extruded out of the pug mill nozzle in a usable condition.

The compaction of the clay causes a denser fired clay body. Compacted clay platelets fuse faster and more completely during the firing than noncompacted platelets. The extruded clay can average 20 percent moisture before it is placed in plastic bags.

Filter Press

Dry clay body formula is mixed with excess water to form liquid slurry. It is then pumped into a series of absorbent leaf-shaped bags. As the bags are compressed, excess water is pressed from the liquid clay. The leaves of moist clay then can go onto the pug mill for further mixing and de-airing. In filter pressing, each clay platelet is effectively surrounded by water in the slurry stage. The water-soaking period produces greater plasticity in the clay than other mixing methods. The filter press procedure is costly and time-consuming for a ceramics supplier to use in producing moist clay. Individual potters would further incur higher production costs using the filter press method.

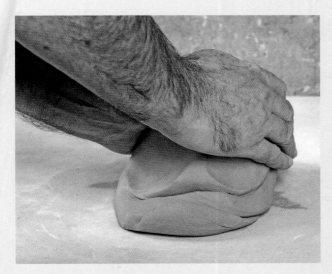
Wedging moist clay on an absorbant surface.

Mixing Tips

First, whether you've mixed your clay yourself or bought it premixed, any clay should be wedged before hand forming or throwing. That's because during pug mill extrusion, the direction of dry clay platelets is changed and disrupted. Wedging clay aligns the clay platelets for forming. As you wedge and discover clay's moisture level, you can make adjustments for softer or harder clay by adding incremental amounts of water or wedging the clay on an absorbent surface to remove excess moisture. Many ceramic pieces fail simply because the potter has not determined the correct moisture content for the specific project.

Second, whether you've mixed the clay yourself or bought it premixed, cover the moist clay completely in plastic and allow it to rest—or age—for several days before any forming operation. After mixing, the moist clay is pliable and plastic and can be bent into shapes. However, each clay platelet is not thoroughly wet, resulting in a lack of plasticity. (Though it's true that filter press clays do wet a higher percentage of clay platelets than other mixing methods.) If you wrap the clay in plastic and allow it to rest, a few days or weeks later, it will have most of the clay platelets saturated and surrounded with water, causing a greater increase in its plasticity.

Buying Premixed Clay

When you buy premixed clay, you let the professionals take charge of what they do best: blend clays with the required amount of water under accurate quality-controlled conditions. Ceramics suppliers should be knowledgeable about the current track record of the contents of their clay body formulas and notice any irregular shipments from the mine. Suppliers want to stay in business and be competitive, so they try to keep their customers satisfied with a good product. By relying on suppliers to do what they do best—mix clay—you can concentrate on producing work to sell or show. The convenience of ordering ready-to-use moist clay cannot be overstated.

Evaluate the Formula

Premixed clay is only as good as the clay body formula and the quality-control practices of the ceramics supplier. An advantage of using a stock clay body is that many potters of various skill levels have already used it with acceptable results. This does not guarantee the clay body will perform well in every situation, but it does indicate better odds of a reliable outcome.

Ceramics suppliers list the stock clay bodies' names along with brief descriptions of handling and firing characteristics in oxidation and reduction atmospheres. Also listed are shrinkage and absorption figures at various temperatures and pyrometric cone ratings. Remember, all descriptive information is gathered from conditions that might not be

A ceramics supplier loads material into an industrial clay mixer. Many studios do not have room for large equipment, so ordering premixed clay is a space saver.

present in your own kiln. Your kiln size and firing cycles can change both shrinkage and absorption rates of the fired clay. Use the catalog description only as a guideline. Before purchasing a stock clay body, ask the supplier for the names of other potters who are using that clay. One or two phone calls will produce more information about the handling and firing qualities of the clay than the brief descriptions in the catalogs.

Quality Control

Buying premixed clay reduces the quality-control aspect to one of monitoring the moist clay as it arrives in the studio. Check each batch for raw color, consistency, and fired results. Most potters do not have the time to take a small sample from each box of clay and fire it. However, any amount of testing before committing to a new load of clay is worth the effort. Here are a few things to keep in mind.

Buying premixed clay means relinquishing some control of the production operation. Because monitoring every aspect of production down to the smallest detail is impossible, the potter should carefully choose the areas where control is critical. Most ceramics suppliers regard their stock clay body formulas as proprietary information and will not reveal exact formulas. When problems with forming or firing occur, the cause can be difficult to track down because the clay body formula is unknown. Reputable suppliers will give any information on bad shipments of clays from the mine or mixing irregularities that might help in resolving the cause of the defect. In many instances, without the clay body formula, it becomes impossible to resolve problems. The potter must decide if the occasional mixing irregularities and loss of control are worth the advantages of premixed clay.

Buying premixed clay means being an informed consumer. Occasionally when a raw material is not readily available, the ceramics supplier will make a substitution. Always ask about any material substitutions before ordering clay. Over the years, many stock clay bodies change so much that very little is left of the original formula. As mines exhaust their supply of clay or, frequently, the clay is present but not economically profitable to mine, substitute clays have to be found. It is a challenge to incorporate the correct substitute into the formula without changing the working properties, fired color, shrinkage, and absorption qualities of the original. Do not assume that because the moist clay body's name stays the same that the formula does also.

Buying premixed clay is relying on another person or company to supply your studio with a vital raw material. As with any cooperative enterprise, problems occur and rational compromises have to be worked out to gain an objective. Some people cannot find a reputable ceramic supplier or do not want to compromise their requirements for moist clay. Continuing to use suppliers' premixed or custom clay bodies in such situations will only cause more problems. In short, some potters and suppliers cannot function together effectively. Recognize this situation, choose another supplier, or make your own clay, but do not remain in a problem-producing cycle.

Buying premixed clay can allow the potter greater flexibility in trying several different stock clay bodies. Many suppliers will give free samples of stock clay to potential customers.

TIP

Timing Clay Orders

Potters often wait to order a new batch of moist clay until their supplies are gone. At this point, production has fallen behind, and you might hurry to make new pieces without testing the clay first. If the new batch is defective, time and money will be lost. Try to time the next clay delivery while old clay is still available, then work the new clay into the firing schedule slowly. This planning will give some measure of insurance because a whole kiln load of work will not be based on a new batch of clay.

CHOOSING A CERAMICS SUPPLIER

Most ceramics suppliers carry a line of clays, ranging from low-temperature, white casting slips to dark stoneware for throwing on the wheel. Specialized blends of clay are frequently available for salt/soda firing, Raku, mid-range porcelain, and slip casting. The appropriate choice for moist premixed clay depends on several factors that are distinctive to each potter: forming method, firing temperature range, kiln atmosphere, glaze, and fired color. Ceramics suppliers usually have several different premixed clays within a given range.

Before you choose a supplier, ask other potters for their recommendations. For example, choosing a supplier that sells low-priced clay but doesn't have a good reputation ultimately can be very expensive, due to improperly mixed clay, random delivery schedules, lack of technical support, and substandard business practices. The price of a stock moist clay or private formula clay is really not relevant; the rate of defects produced by a given batch of clay is. (Ceramics suppliers for the most part do not keep these types of records, or if they do, they don't tell this to customers. However, other potters can relay their experience with a particular clay, helping you choose a clay body with a good result for others.)

Establishing a good professional relationship with your supplier has several benefits. The ceramics supply company's sales and technical staff can be an added help in obtaining information about premixed clays. They can offer advice on how other potters are using the clay and supply information on dry clays that are available for use in private clay body formulas.

Another thing to keep in mind when buying premixed clay is that your shipping costs will be lower from a supplier that is nearby. But keep in mind, the overriding consideration when choosing a ceramics supplier is not the cost or delivery charge, but the quality of the clay. Any small savings in choosing a clay just for its low price can be a negated if the clay formula is not sound or the mixing procedures inaccurate.

Ordering Moist Clay

If you choose a local clay supplier, visit the clay mixing operation. This is a valuable opportunity to determine how seriously a ceramics supplier regards the clay mixing part of the business. Simple observations lend significant clues. Are the clay storage and mixing areas reasonably clean and well organized? Do the people mixing clay appear motivated and knowledgeable? Are any special cleaning procedures enacted when mixing white clays or porcelain? (They are easily contaminated with non-white firing clays.) What quality control measures are taken when different clay body recipes are mixed?

If you are not satisfied with your observations, look for another supplier.

Order Early and Often

Always reorder moist clay when only half of your current supply is exhausted. This will allow an opportunity to randomly test fire the new clay while you are still using a proven batch of old clay.

Also, keep careful records for each batch of clay, noting the production code on each box. A shipment containing several batches may have more than one production code. Most suppliers package moist clay in 50-pound (22.7-kg) boxes that contain two 25-pound (11-kg) bags of clay. The clay is packed in plastic bags, which are semi-permeable, and air will begin to harden the clay within a few months. Check the moisture content of clay in plastic bags periodically to ensure it has not hardened. If it has, spray some water on the clay and reseal the plastic bags. You might have to repeat this procedure several times to achieve a higher moisture content in the clay and a softer clay.

Report Problems Immediately

If you have problems with the premixed clay, report them immediately to the supplier, listing the production code and a description of the fault, and be prepared to send a sample of the defect for evaluation. Do not continue to use a clay—or any product for that matter—once you have encountered a problem, because this can constitute acceptance.

As a standard business policy, ceramics suppliers have limited liability on dry and moist clay, which means, at best, they will only replace the product if it is defective. Suppliers will not replace kilns, shelves, or posts damaged by defective clay. Nor will they compensate you for lost time or potential sales caused by defective clay.

Keep in mind that suppliers will replace clay only if it can be proven the clay was at fault and you did not cause the defect through improper forming, glazing, or firing.

Shrinkage and Absorption in Moist Clays

Obtain information on how the clay will look at your particular firing temperature and kiln atmosphere. The supplier will provide premixed moist clay descriptions, photos, and small sample chips of the fired clay.

Suppliers also publish shrinkage and absorption percentages for every moist clay they sell. Shrinkage and absorption percentages can give an indication of how a clay reacts when fired to its maturating range, but the percentages are most useful when comparing different moist clays fired in the same kiln.

Remember, these statistics are based on how the clay shrinks and absorbs water in the ceramics supplier's kiln, not yours. For the same reason, do not compare one company's shrinkage and absorption figures with another's.

So for example, if you mistakenly fire a cone 06 (1,828°F [998°C]) clay body to cone 10 (2,345°F [1,285°C]), it is unlikely you will receive a free replacement batch of clay.

Private Clay Formulas

When you buy premixed clay, you might discover that no ceramics suppliers' stock clay bodies meet your specific needs. Perhaps you need a private clay formula, a formula designed just for you. Some suppliers offer the value-added service. You find or create a clay body formula, which the ceramics supplier will then mix.

Bear in mind that when a supplier mixes a private formula, the supplier does not assume any responsibility for potential defects caused by the formula. You must feel confident that the private formula clay will work in the following respects: forming method, kiln atmosphere, glaze interaction, temperature range, and fired color.

Because it is not economical for a supplier to mix up a small test batch of private formula clay, there is usually a minimum amount required to fill the order, which can range from 1,000 to 2,000 pounds (about 450 to 900 kg). If a supplier mixes a small test batch, be prepared to pay for this special service. The fee is well worth it, because a ton of untested clay can be a very expensive test. If your supplier doesn't offer to sell you a test batch, mix your own test batch before committing to a larger quantity.

CLAY BODY FORMULAS

Clays that are formulated and mixed by potters or sold by ceramic supply companies are called clay bodies. A clay body is a combination of clays, fluxes, and fillers. Each serves a function to help determine forming characteristics, drying shrinkage, surface texture, fired absorption, fired shrinkage, glaze interface, and fired clay color.

Clay body formulas, as in cake-baking recipes, can encompass subtle variations, which bring distinctive forming and firing characteristics to the whole mix. For example, if a medium- to high-temperature clay body requires flux to help bring other materials in the clay body into a melt, there are many types of feldspar that could fill that requirement. However, you must decide which of the available feldspars will be appropriate for the clay body. The best clay body formulas contain appropriate raw materials and the correct ratios of clays, fluxes, and fillers to achieve their desired result.

The use of metallic coloring oxides such as manganese dioxide, iron oxide, chrome oxide, and cobalt oxide can produce a black clay.

In a white clay body, cobalt oxide can produce a blue clay.

In a white clay body, chrome oxide can produce a green clay.

For a list of common clay body formulas, see Appendix II, page 154.

Types of Clays

Clay, the first of the three essential ingredients of a clay body, is grouped depending on refractory qualities, particle size, oxide composition, loss on ignition, shrinkage rates, absorption rates, and other defining characteristics. The basic clay groups found in clay body formulas are fireclays, ball clays, kaolins, stoneware clays, bentonites, and earthenware clays. We'll go into further detail about ball and fireclays below.

Understand that not every clay group will be used in every clay body formula. For example, some earthenware clays, due to their relatively high iron content and low maturing range, would not be found in porcelain clay body formulas, which require low-iron-content, refractory kaolins to achieve their white fired color.

Within each major group of clays are subgroups that further define a particular clay characteristic, such as plastic kaolin (such as grolleg clay) and non-plastic kaolin (such as English China clay). Further, each group and sub-group contains many individual brand names of clay. Some of the many ball clays are Tennessee ball clay #9, Taylor ball clay, Kentucky ball clay OM #4, Zamek ball clay, Kentucky Special, and Thomas ball clay.

Each group of ball clays, stoneware clays, kaolins, bentonites, fireclays, and earthenware clays contributes specific attributes to the total clay body formula. Those qualities include particle size, green strength, fired strength, fired color, shrinkage, plasticity, deflocculating potential (also known as Zeta potential), texture, forming abilities, and low amounts of warping in drying and firing stages.

Ball Clays

Ball clays are characterized by their plasticity. The small platelet or particle-size structure of ball clays imparts great plasticity to the clay in the moist state. However, ball clays require large amounts of water to achieve plasticity. Plasticity and water can result in dry shrinkage, fired shrinkage, and warping. That's one reason why ball clays are not the sole component in any clay body formula. Another reason is because they can contain elevated amounts of carbonaceous matter, which aid in plasticity but can lead to burn-out problems in firing stages. Burn out is when carbonaceous matter is trapped in the clay body and begins causing carbon deposits in the clay body.

Ball clay is one component of a clay body formula that can contain other types of clays, including feldspar, flint, and other raw materials. The raw materials determine the clay's eventual forming method, firing temperature, and fired color.

Relative Sizes of Clay Particles

| Fireclay | Stoneware Clay | Ball Clay | Bentonites |

Bentonites and ball clays have the smallest platelet size, followed by stoneware clays, kaolins, and fire-clays. Earthenware clays can vary in platelet size depending on their individual location and the geologic forces used in their formulation. Generally, the platelet diameter of clays can range from 100 microns to 0.1 micron. (1 micron = $1/24,500$ of an inch.)

Several common types of ball clay are used in clay body and glaze formulas. There are variations in particle-size distribution, organic content, and chemical makeup, along with other variables throughout this group. However, each clay has a data sheet that can offer information on its eventual use in clay bodies and glazes. Data sheets can be obtained through the clay mine or ceramics supplier. Ball clays vitrify at approximately 2,000°F to 2,200°F (1,093°C to 1,204°C).

FINE BALL CLAYS

A typical data sheet listing ball clays will indicate which clays have finer or coarser particle size distributions. Particle size can be charted on a graph, giving a fingerprint (or unique formula) for each ball clay. The distribution can be complex because all clays have particles as large as 100 microns and as small as 0.1 microns (1 micron = 1/24,500 of an inch). The number of particles in each range deter-mines the overall fineness or coarseness of the clay.

Fine ball clays have greater plasticity and increased strength when dry, which makes them suitable for plastic-forming operations, such as throwing and hand build-ing. Finer clays can tighten a clay body structure, causing an exothermic reaction (releasing heat), preventing the

oxidation of organic matter when heated in the 572° to 932°F (300° to 500°C) temperature range.

COARSE BALL CLAYS

Coarse ball clays are less plastic and better suited for casting slip clay formulas. Coarser ball clays allow water to "wick" through the liquid clay into the mold, building up an acceptable clay thickness in the cast piece. Coarse particle–size ball clays also allow the clay body to "firm" quickly, or develop durability after draining out the excess slip from the mold. The leather-hard piece can be handled faster when it is taken out of the mold. Coarser ball clays will contribute to greater durability and firmness in a cast piece when it is removed from the plaster mold.

Coarse ball clays also can be used in clay bodies that do not require the degree of plasticity needed in throwing bodies. Larger particle-size ball clay can be used in hand building, coil, Ram press, or dry press forming clay bodies.

BALL CLAYS FOR HAND BUILDING AND SCULPTURE

The percentage of ball clay used in a clay body formula is directly related to the forming process. Ball clays are often

Greater amounts of ball clay in a clay body formula can negatively affect the mixture in the following ways.

- Excessive dry shrinkage, fired shrinkage, and warping during firing/drying

- Cracking where thin and thick sections meet
- Unequal shrinkage and stress cracks, because thin sections dry faster than thick areas
- Moist clay that is sticky and deforms under pressure during the forming process
- Gelatinous quality that is difficult to shape

used to increase a clay body's plastic qualities. The goal is to use enough ball clay for the required degree of plasticity needed. The amount and type of ball clay used in hand building and sculpture clay bodies will depend on several factors, such as the forming method (coil, clay slab construction, pinch construction), clay body fired color, and the clay bodies fired shrinkage and absorption rates.

The amount of ball clay used in hand building or sculpture bodies can range from 1 to 15 percent. Clay bodies intended for Ram press or dry press operations, where the clay is compressed by hydraulic forming action between molds, do not require significant percentages of ball clay. Because of the pressure put on clay during these forming processes, the clay body does not need to be especially plastic.

CLAYS FOR THROWING

Ball clay adds much-needed plasticity to throwing clay bodies. The amount and type of ball clay used in throwing bodies can vary, depending on other clays in the formula, such as fireclays or stoneware clays. It can also depend on other ceramic materials in the formula, including feldspar, flint, talc, or grog. Generally, the percentage of ball clay in throwing bodies can be as low as 5 percent or as high as 30 percent of the total clay body formula.

When ball clay is not balanced with other materials in the clay body formula, your thrown pots will suffer. In higher percentages, ball clay can result in the moist body taking on water too fast when it is being thrown on the wheel. Excessive ball clay also can cause thixotropy, or deformation under pressure, as your fingers manipulate the form. The moist clay body may sag or sink, resulting in the inability to pull up tall forms on the wheel.

BALL CLAYS IN GLAZE

Ball clays supply silica and alumina to glaze formulas, affecting raw glaze fit, glaze maturation temperature, glaze opacity, and glaze surface texture. Ball clays or other small "plate" structure clays, such as bentonites, help glaze materials stay

Moist clay can lack plasticity, which is often revealed by cracking along the edges when a slab of clay is rolled out.

in suspension. However, in some glaze formulas that require a clay component, ball clays can cause a clear glaze to fire semi-opaque or cloudy because they contain higher amounts of iron and manganese compared to kaolins, which are also used in glaze formulas. However, in opaque or colored glaze formulas, the metallic oxide concentrations in ball clays generally do not affect a work's fired appearance.

BALL CLAYS IN CASTING SLIPS

Most casting slip formulas consist of 35 to 50 percent ball clay. Coarser particle-size ball clays are better suited for slip casting than finer particle-size clays because they allow a thicker wall section to build in the mold. Ball clays in casting slips contribute green strength and plasticity in the pouring and drying stages. Green strength is the property that allows the piece to resist mechanical shock. Plasticity is required in the casting process from the moment the body begins to shrink until the point it reaches the bone-dry stage. Some potters argue that plasticity remains even in the dry state and allows the piece to flex a little instead of breaking.

Fireclays

Another common clay found in clay body formulas is fireclay, named such because it is primarily associated with fire or heat. Fireclay contributes to particle-size variation, enhancing a clay body's forming characteristics. Fireclays enable the clay body to withstand high-temperature pyroplastic deformation, which can result in the clay body slumping, bloating, or fusing to the kiln shelf. Potters use fireclays in diverse ceramic products, such as floor and wall tiles, functional pottery, and sculptures.

However, fireclays should be carefully examined before adding them to a clay body formula. Fireclays are more likely to cause problems in the forming, drying, and glazing processes than ball clays and others, such as stoneware.

Fireclays are refractory and are able to withstand deformation temperatures above 3,000°F (1,648°C).

FIRECLAY CONSISTENCY

Platelet-size distribution simply means how many small, medium, or large platelets are in a clay. The distribution of platelet sizes affects the texture, or "tooth," of the moist clay during forming operations. The shape of the platelets, their direction in relation to each other, and the colloidal water adhesion forces that bind them together also play a part in determining the handling characteristics of the moist clay.

Platelet-size distribution can influence plastic qualities, shrinkage rate, forming potential, and drying characteristics. Fireclay with a greater percentage of larger platelets will produce a clay body formula that is less plastic with decreased ability to bend when moist. Fireclays with a finer platelet size shrink more, have greater plasticity when moist, and take longer to dry. Mixing fireclay with feldspars, flint, and grog can mitigate fireclay platelet-size distribution side effects.

CONTAMINANTS IN FIRECLAYS

Fireclays are the weakest link of the clays in a clay body formula because of contaminants, including carbonaceous materials such as lignite, peat, coal, and other associated tramp materials. Fireclays can also contain inconsistently sized particles of silica, iron, and manganese.

Technically, all of these negative (or unpredictable) qualities can be refined out of the clay. But fireclay is most often used by steel mills, casting foundries, and brick manufacturers, which can use the material with minimal processing in their forming processes. Potters represent less than one-tenth of a percent of sales. Therefore, manufacturers may not concentrate on filtering out impurities that cause problems in pottery forming.

The following contaminants are prevalent in fireclay.

Iron: Potters want small, random brown specks (0.5 mm to 1 mm in diameter) in the fired clay body. However, large nodules of iron (4 to 6 mm in diameter) in the fired body can cause outsized brown blemishes.

Manganese: Fireclays also can contain aggregate lumps of manganese, which can cause brown/black concave or convex defects in fired clay surfaces.

Lime: Nodules of lime can expand in the fired clay body as it takes on atmospheric moisture. The resulting half moon–shaped cracks in the fired clay body disrupt the surface. Lime nodules or gypsum formed alongside seams of fireclay or in pockets contained in the clay seam can range from pebble to fist size and can result in a clay body defect called lime pop. (See "Lime Pop" on page 72.)

Silica: The larger particles of silica in fireclay that convert to cristobalite will produce a larger expansion/contraction, exerting a greater pressure on the body during firing and cooling than small particles. Seemingly intact functional pottery with a buildup of cristobalite can crack later when heated in a hot kitchen oven due to cristobalite inversion in a similar cooling range. Cracks can occur anywhere on the pot and have a sharp edge, as though hit by a hammer.

Earthenware clays

Earthenware clays are characterized by their porosity between cone 010 and cone 02 (1,657°F-2,016°F [903°C-1,102°C]). They can have high levels of organic material, which may cause the raw color to appear gray, green, or black even though they fire white or off-white. Some earthenware clay deposits have high levels of iron, which can fire to red or brown. Their particle size range and the plastic qualities vary depending on the individual deposit.

Stoneware clays

Stoneware clays have a medium platelet size compared to the fine platelets of ball clays and the large platelets of fireclays. They are fairly plastic, and they have refractory qualities slightly below those of fireclays. They mature at a temperature between cone 6 and cone 12 (1,222°F-2,383°F [661°C-1,306°C]). Stoneware clays vary in raw color, fired color, and plasticity. They compose a large percentage of high-temperature clay body formulas.

Kaolin clays

Kaolin clays have low iron content and are known for their purity and their white fired color. They are formed by the decomposition of feldspathic rock and are found in pockets rather than seams. Kaolins are very refractory, melting at temperatures higher than 3,200°F (1,760°C). They have a coarse grain that exhibits low shrinkage rates and little plasticity. As a group, kaolins are frequently used in porcelain clay body formulas.

Bentonites

Bentonites are the most plastic clays, have the smallest platelet size, and are formed by the weathering of volcanic glass.

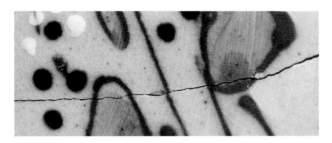

This sharp-edged cooling crack in ware was caused by cristobalite inversion in the kiln. The larger part of the crack (right side) is where the crack started to form.

The chemical composition of fireclays can change from one shipment to the next. Fireclays can contain nodules of chalcopyrite ($CuFeS_2$) and erubescite (Cu_5FeS_4), releasing copper, which can cause green specks in the fired clay body.

Due to their small particle size, they have high shrinkage rates and can have high dry strength. Small additions of bentonite (1% to 2% based on the dry weight of the clay body) can increase the plastic properties of the clay body.

Fluxes

Fluxes are the second component of a clay body formula, and they are responsible for lowering the melting point of heat-resistant clays and fillers. Flux helps a clay body melt in a predetermined maturing range. In functional pottery, the maturing range occurs when absorption, shrinkage, and fired color are compatible with the glaze, producing a dense, vitreous nonabsorbent clay body.

Every temperature range has the appropriate choice of flux materials that will work compatibly with the raw materials and clays contained within the clay body. If a low-melting flux is used in a high-temperature clay body, the result is over-vitrification. An over-fluxed clay body can bloat, slump, shrink excessively, and fuse to the kiln shelves.

Feldspars are the best flux for clay bodies in medium- to high-temperature ranges (above cone 6, 2,232°F [1,222°C]). The three basic groups of feldspars used in ceramics are soda feldspars, potash feldspars, and lithium feldspars. Within the three groups, many individual feldspars can be chosen for a clay body formula. A beneficial quality of feldspars in medium- to high-temperature clay body formulas is their ability to enter into a melt slowly over a wide temperature range. Talc is sometimes used in stoneware clay bodies, but it can have active and fast melting characteristics if used in inappropriate amounts.

TIP

Mesh Size

The mesh size of the screen is a factor in determining the amount of contaminants that are allowed to pass through with the fireclay. A large, 20x mesh screen can allow greater quantities of tramp material or contaminants (twigs, stones, coal, or processing debris such as bolts, wire, and metal parts) to enter the final bag of clay. A smaller, 50x mesh screen that traps more contaminants will produce higher-quality fireclay.

Fillers

Fillers, the third clay body component, reduce clay body shrinkage and warping in the drying and firing stages. The most widely used fillers include flint, pyrophyllite, silica sand, sawdust, mullite, calcined kaolin, kyanite, calcined alumina, and grogs of various sizes. The amount of filler used in a clay body formula depends on how you will form the clay. For example, clay bodies designed for slab forming and tile making usually have more filler or non-plastic material than throwing bodies. But, as with anything, there is a happy medium for fillers. If the amount of filler is too high, the clay body's plastic qualities are decreased.

Flint as a filler is often called a "glass former" and needs high temperatures (3,200°F [1,760°C]) to melt by itself. But when flint is combined with a flux, its melting temperature decreases. Flint reduces dry shrinkage and warping in the clay body. It also promotes glaze fit by contracting the clay body to match the contraction of the covering glaze layer.

Clay Body Characteristics

Before mixing a clay body formula, it is important to first decide what parameters and conditions the clay body will encounter. Formulas can fail due to the inappropriate use of raw materials or an unsuitable use of the clay body formula. For example, a clay body formula using only ball clay, which is very plastic, can shrink, warp, and crack excessively in the drying and firing stages. Or, when a frit (low-melting glaze or clay body flux) is used in a medium- to high-temperature clay body, excessive glass formation can occur, along with slumping, bloating, and other defects in the fired ware.

Your first job is to decide on the correct mix of materials for your clay body. You do this by asking what characteristics will be essential in the clay body. Then, develop a list of criteria so you can choose the best raw materials for your application.

As you decide on raw materials for your clay body formula, ask these questions.

Wheel-Thrown Jar, 8½" (21 cm) tall, 8" (20.3 cm) diameter, Firing: cone 9 (2,300°F [1,260°C]), salt-fired
See page 165 for formula

What is your forming method? Potter's wheel, slab construction, slip casting, Ram pressed, dry pressed, jiggered, or extruded—each method will require a specific combination of raw materials. For example, clay bodies used on the potter's wheel will require higher percentages of plastic ball clays compared to dry-pressed clay bodies, where the extreme hydraulic pressure of the press forms the object. Slip-casting clay bodies will require a deflocculating component, such as sodium silicate or Darvan #7—soluble electrolytes that create clay that can be poured. Some clay bodies can be used for more than one forming method; however, it is unusual to achieve optimum performance in each forming method.

What color do you prefer for fired clay? White clay bodies can be developed into yellow, blue, green, or other colors with the addition of body stains or metallic coloring oxides. Clay bodies that originate as brown can be developed into dark brown or black with the addition of high iron-bearing clays or metallic coloring oxides.

How hot will your kiln get? Clay bodies will act differently when heated. In functional ware it is preferable that the pottery holds water and be nonabsorbent.

What is your kiln atmosphere? A clay body can be formulated for oxidation, neutral, or reduction kiln atmospheres. In oxidation atmospheres, the air-to-fuel ratio is higher, causing a cleaner ignition to the fuel. In neutral kiln atmospheres, there is an equal air-to-fuel ratio. In reduction kiln atmospheres, the fuel-to-air ratio is greater, causing carbon monoxide to pull oxygen from the oxides contained in clay and glaze. In reduction kiln atmospheres, metallic oxides such as iron and manganese tend to flux the clay or glaze to a greater degree. Each atmosphere can influence the fired color, density, glaze interaction, and surface quality of the clay.

How available are raw materials? Before you develop a clay body formula (on paper), be sure all raw materials are available. Check with suppliers to ensure they still stock the feldspar you're seeking or the ball clay you want. In such a case, ask suppliers for logical substitutions for discontinued materials.

Clay Body at Work

Clay bodies are designed for various functions, including the following:

Sculpture: large scale and/or thick cross sections, low shrinkage and warping

Freeze/thaw conditions: allowing for expansion and contraction

Wood-fired kiln effects: shows random flashing effects of ash deposits on ware

Soda/salt effects: unglazed areas of clay reveal a glossy "orange peel" surface texture

Once-fired or raw glazing: clay allows for a compatible glaze fit and single firing

Porcelain: white clay color, translucent when thin

Flame ware: clay body exposed to direct flame in use

Functional pottery: durable, nonabsorbent, compatible with a wide range of glazes, can be used in indirect flame situations

Slip casting: a fluid clay that can be poured into plaster molds

Ram press: a clay body that can be formed by the hydraulic action of the press

Jigger/jolleying: a clay body that can be formed when a template is drawn against a spinning mold

Dry press: a low-moisture clay body formulated for extreme hydraulic pressure forming

TIP
Test Kilns

When increasing the flux component of a clay body formula, always shape test pieces and place them in a regular production kiln on top of an old kiln shelf. Firing clay and glazes in small test kilns can produce inaccurate results. Smaller kilns have faster firing and cooling cycles and less thermal mass compared to larger production kilns. In order to accurately conduct testing, it is important to reproduce the heating and cooling cycles in any kiln firing.

Clay Plasticity

Two important factors determine moist clay's plasticity: the individual clay body formula and the amount of time it spends in the moist state. The forming process you plan to use (throwing, hand building, etc.) will determine how plastic your clay must be. You can increase clay plasticity with the following additives.

Bentonite: Bentonites are an extremely plastic group of clays, and they can enhance the working qualities of the clay body. Bentonites have very small platelet structures, which physically touch larger platelet structure clays in the moist mix. The small platelet size of bentonites also increases the water-film bonding of the entire clay water structure.

As a rule, never exceed 2 percent bentonite in a clay body. Otherwise, the clay body will become gummy when used on the wheel or in other forming operations.

Ball clay: Ball clays also have small platelet structures that increase the surface areas touching other clays and raw materials in the clay mix. Ball clays also increase the colloidal film action in the clay body.

Be sure that ball clay is less than 25 percent of your total clay body formula. Otherwise, the moist clay will take on water at a faster rate during the throwing process, resulting in the clay slumping and sagging during the last stages of forming on the wheel. (For more on ball clay, see page 47.)

Mold and other organic agents: Most types of mold growth in moist clay can increase plasticity because it augments the binding action and attraction of clay platelets. Enhancing the film of water between each clay platelet with mold will increase the clay-to-clay attraction. One recipe to encourage mold growth in clay starts by mixing a 100-pound (45.4-kg) batch of clay formula. Add $^1/_2$ cup (118 ml) of beer, coffee, or apple cider vinegar, or 3 ounces (85 g) of yeast to start mold growth in the clay/water mixture.

Depending on the pH level of the clay-mixing water, the individual clay's organic matter, and the studio temperature conditions, mold can grow on the surface of moist clay. Most types of mold are beneficial, increasing the plastic properties of the clay. Simply wedging the clay will evenly disperse the mold.

However, if you keep moist clay long enough in a warm, dark place, it will grow mold without any additional organic materials being added to the mix.

Epsom salts: Adding Epsom salts (magnesium sulfate) will increase the attraction of clay platelets in the moist clay state, causing the clay to become flocculated. Add 5 ounces (142 g) of Epsom salt for every 100 pounds (45.4 kg) of dry clay formula (0.3 percent). Add Epsom salts to water before mixing with clay so it disperses efficiently. Clay platelets will draw together just like north and south poles of a magnet. The overall effect is a tight, plastic clay body with good throwing properties.

> Note: Excessive levels of Epsom salts can cause salt migration to the drying clay surface, which will create a white powdery coating. The salt can result in blistering and carbon trapping in the fired clay.

Additive A: Additive A is a blend of water-soluble lignosulphonates and organic/inorganic chemicals that is a byproduct of the paper manufacturing process. When used in amounts of $1/16$ to $1/8$ percent of the dry weight of the clay, Additive A can increase moist clay plasticity without changing its fired shrinkage, absorption, or clay color. Additive A is produced in several versions, some of which contain barium in a safe, nontoxic form. Additive A in barium versions can eliminate scumming, which can occur when moist clay body begins to dry, carrying soluble salts to exposed clay surfaces. The soluble salt layer (scumming) can fuse at high temperatures, creating a glass-like irregular surface on the clay. When glaze is applied over the scumming area, it can result in a glaze defect such as blistering.

(See page 107.) Any type of Additive A, when used in a clay body, will increase plasticity and green strength without causing excessive shrinkage rates in the drying and firing stages, as with excessive additions of ball clay.

Water and Plasticity

The chemical composition of the water used in mixing the clay body can alter the plastic properties of the moist clay. The amount of water required to form the clay into a plastic mass is called the water of plasticity. The percentage of water required can vary with the individual clays and raw materials contained within the clay body. Some clay bodies, due to their high percentage of ball clay (small platelet sizes), might require 40 percent more water for plasticity than clay bodies containing higher levels of coarse fireclays (large platelet sizes). Stoneware clay body formulas require only 25 percent water.

If the water contains soluble salts of sodium or calcium, they can migrate to the clay surface in the drying stage, causing an irregular surface interfering with the subsequent glaze application. The soluble material forms a glaze, which can result in blistering and carbon trapping. Household water softeners can introduce sodium into the mixing water, which can alter the handling qualities of the moist clay body. Sodium also can cause deflocculating characteristics in the moist clay, resulting in very soft clay under forming pressure. Although the chemical composition of the water has a larger effect on slip casting clay bodies, do not overlook discoloration or soluble salt crystals that can occur when the clay body is drying. Also note whether the moist clay is too soft or rubbery in forming stages.

> Note: Generally, the standard percentage of water by weight found in moist plastic clay bodies used on the potter's wheel or in hand building is 20 percent.

TIP

Raw Material Substitutions

When a clay or raw material is not available, choose a substitute from the same group of clays as the original. Fireclays, ball clays, stoneware clays, bentonites, kaolins, and earthenware are all common clay groups. The three basic groups of feldspar are sodium based, potassium based and lithium based. A feldspar substitution should come from the original feldspar grouping.

When possible, always test a one-for-one substitution. If this does not work, you'll have to recalculate the clay body formula.

Mining Clay

To get an idea of where, exactly, clay comes from, let's take a photographic tour through Christy Minerals, located 50 miles (80.5 km) west of St. Louis, Missouri. This mine uses selective open-pit excavation to extract Hawthorn Bond fireclay. The top layer of overburden is taken away and the clay seam exposed. After carefully removing the clay, it is stockpiled and weathered for twelve to eighteen months, causing it to break down. The natural freeze/thaw conditions plus rain and sun hydrate and dehydrate the clay platelets, ultimately improving consistency and plasticity.

The clay is then transported to the plant, where it is dried and placed in a covered shed until it is ground to the appropriate mesh size. There are several grinding methods, depending on the desired grain size and distribution of the product. Finally, the material is tested for particle size distribution and placed in packaging ranging from 50- and 100-pound (22.7- and 45.4-kg) paper bags to larger 3,500-pound (1,588-kg) super sacks.

Raw clay is rarely taken from the mine site without some form of processing. More than 99 percent of clays are used by industrial and commercial sectors. Potters represent less than 1 percent of the total market, and their limited role affects the quality of clays they can purchase. Clays for commercial applications require a degree of uniformity and quality control, but not necessarily the same kind of processing that potters demand. Two machines used in the preparation of raw clay are the roller mill and the hammer mill.

This exposed clay face shows overburden on top. The surface material—such as soil, branches, shrubs and other covering—is removed, exposing the various seams of clay.

Notice the different qualities of clay and higher-iron-content seams on top. Depending on the geological formation of the clay pit, the various levels can contain clays having different mineral, organic particle size, and tramp material content.

Mining clay for movement to processing plant. A careful survey of the clay field is made, plotting the different layers of clay. After that, clay is excavated from the various pits in a very precise manner and then taken to the processing plant.

The Roller Mill Process

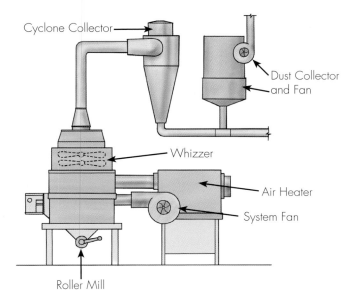

Cyclone Collector

Dust Collector and Fan

Whizzer

Air Heater

System Fan

Roller Mill

During the roller mill operation, some free moisture is removed from the clay and fed between a ring and a series of spinning rolls. Clay is ground and dried, then thrown between the ring and rolls. A stream of air lifts the finer clay particles up to a whizzer (fan blades). The faster the blades spin, the finer the clay particles need to be to pass through the whizzer. Once through the whizzer, the clay/air stream goes to a cyclone collector, where the clay is separated from air during the air-floating process. The clay then goes to a packer, where it is bagged and ready for shipment. Greenstripe is an example of a roller-milled air-floated fireclay.

The Hammer Mill Process

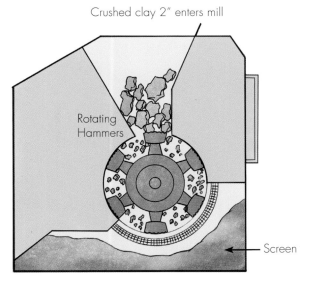

Crushed clay 2" enters mill

Rotating Hammers

Screen

Pulverized clay exits through screens

Clay crushed into 2-inch (5-cm) bits and smaller enter the hammer mill. Hammers rotate and pulverize the clay, which is then pushed through screens at the bottom of the mill. Screen size determines the mesh size of the clay and the size of possible contaminants processed with the clay. Hawthorn bond is an example of a hammer-milled fireclay.

TESTING CLAY BODY FORMULAS

Many potters, from novice hobbyists to veteran ceramic artists, have made the mistake of mixing a large quantity of clay from a given formula without testing a small batch.

Once you choose a clay body formula, mix an appropriate amount of moist clay for shrinkage and absorption testing. Ten pounds (4.5 kg) of dry clay body formula should yield approximately 12 pounds (5.4 kg) of moist clay. This will make six clay test bars, measuring 5" x 2$\frac{1}{2}$" x $\frac{1}{4}$" thick (12.7 cm x 6.4 cm x 6 mm), allowing for plenty leftover for forming sample pots. These pots are then used for a test firing. It's better to create larger test pieces that give a more accurate representation of the clay body. Also, test the clay in multiple firings with many glaze combinations to ensure the clay body formula's reliability.

Test firings will ensure that the raw materials in your clay body act as planned. We discussed earlier the problems that adding too much or too little of a material can present during the firing/heating process—or during forming, for that matter. Not every kiln produces an even atmosphere or temperature. Placing test pieces in various locations within the kiln will offer an accurate indication of the clay body temperature range and color variation caused by the kiln atmosphere.

Fired clay bars ready for an absorption test

Testing for Freeze/Thaw Conditions

When ceramic forms are placed in freeze/thaw conditions, they can fracture and spall (chip due to internal stress). Think of what happens when you leave a favorite flowerpot outdoors during winter. Strong environmental forces are at work, and the pot cracks as a result. Why do clay bodies exposed in more temperate climates remain stable and intact? What are the factors causing freeze/thaw failures, and how can we eliminate them?

Most materials shrink when frozen. However, water expands because of the formation of ice crystals. The open-pore structure of fired clay traps atmospheric moisture by capillary action, in the form of rain, snow, and humidity. Upon freezing, ice crystals expand in the confined, unyielding pore structure of the clay, causing cracking or chipping.

You can use a few different methods to determine a clay body's likelihood to crack, and therefore leak, in freeze/thaw conditions: the Standard Absorption Test, the American Society for Testing and Materials (ASTM) test, or a simple pinch-pot test, which is a less-formal method. We'll talk about each of these in turn.

This earthenware flower pot cracked because of freeze/thaw conditions.

Moisture retained in the fired clay can come from water in the atmosphere, from the pottery being used in a dishwasher, and from any cleaning procedure. Moisture can also accumulate in clay bodies that are used to store food or liquids. As stated, if a clay body contains the appropriate materials and is fired to its maturity, it can have a low absorption percentage or zero-percent absorption and will not subsequently leak. It's important to note that the relationship between clay body shrinkage/absorption and glaze fit determines if a glaze will be stable once it is fired on a clay body.

Testing Kiln Atmosphere

With hydrocarbon-based fuels (natural gas, propane, wood, oil, coal, sawdust), the kiln can be manipulated to produce oxidation, neutral, and various intensities of reduction kiln atmospheres, all of which can affect clay body color. Oxidation atmosphere in hydrocarbon-based fueled kilns can cause variations in clay body color when compared to oxidation atmospheres produced in electric kilns. This is because of impurities in the hydrocarbon-based fuel and water vapor present during the combustion process. Reduction kiln atmospheres also can cause increased clay body vitrification, because the metallic coloring oxides contained in the clay body are subjected to increased melting.

In electric kilns, the uniform oxidation atmosphere causes little or no variation in clay body color. Still, temperature variations could affect shrinkage and absorption of the fired clay body. Higher temperatures can flux (melt) metallic coloring oxides in the clay body, causing darker fired colors along with increased vitrification.

Standard Absorption Test

This test measures the percentage of water entering a fired clay body when it is soaked and boiled in water. This test replicates how the clay body will react in natural freeze/thaw environments. During this test, the open pores of the clay body absorb water. The clay is soaked in water for 24 hours, then boiled in water for 5 hours.

Consistency of the technique when performing this test is vital to arriving at an accurate absorption rate. The same person should conduct each clay's test, and the test should be repeated to check the results. The absorption percentage should be the same for each test.

Equipment

- Fired test clay bars
- Scale accurate to $\frac{1}{100}$ of a gram
- Container to boil water
- Calculator
- Damp, lint-free towel
- Metal pin stilt
- Pins
- Container

Instructions

① Make at least five test bars that are $^3/_8''$ (10 mm) thick, 1″ (2.5 cm) wide, and 5″ (12.7 cm) long from the same clay you will use for your outdoor ceramics project. Averaging the absorption percentage of several bars will ensure testing accuracy. The bars should be free of cracks, indentations, or surface blemishes that could trap water when the fired clay surface is dry. Round the edges of the bars to prevent chipping. Any small change in weight from imperfections can result in a significant error in the final calculation. To ensure accuracy, space out the bars and fire them in the same kiln, selecting the identical kiln firing cycle and stacking arrangement you will use with your project.

② After firing the test bars, each bar is placed on the scale and carefully weighed. The exact amount is written on a notepad.

③ Place the test tile on pins inside a container, then fill with tepid water. Soak the test bar for 24 hours. Then, wipe off the tile with a damp, lint-free towel. Carefully weigh the test tile.

④ Now, boil the tile for 5 hours. Use a large enough container so the water does not boil off. Also, check the boiling water level periodically to ensure water is present in the container. Wipe the tile off again with the damp, lint-free towel. Carefully weigh the tile and record the measurement.

⑤ Calculate the absorption percentage by using the following formula:

[wet weight − dry weight]/dry weight = absorption percentage of 24-hour soaking absorption

[wet weight − dry weight]/dry weight = absorption percentage of 5-hour boiled water absorption

Compare the percentages between the 24-hour soaking absorption and the 5-hour boiled water absorption:

24-hour soaking absorption percentage/5-hour boiling absorption percentage = the ratio of soaking absorption to boiled water absorption

The above calculation, the absorption rate, should be less than .78 percent, which would make it safe for freeze/thaw conditions.

FOR EXAMPLE:

(96 g [wet weight] − 93 g [dry weight])/93 g [dry weight] = 0.03 or 3%

(97 g [wet weight] − 93 g [dry weight])/93 g [dry weight] = 0.04 or 4%

0.03 divided by 0.04 = .75

This absorption testing procedure used by the ASTM is as effective as the standard test described earlier.

Step ① Fired clay bars lined up for an absorption test. It is always best to test more than one bar and use the average absorption percentage for a more precise calculation.

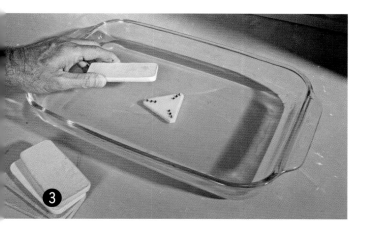

Step ③ Place the test tile on pins inside a container, then fill with tepid water. Soak the test bar for 24 hours.

Step ④ Boil the tile for 5 hours. Carefully dry each test bar before weighing

TIP

Absorbency and Porosity

Two terms that are frequently used interchangeably but describe different conditions are absorbency and porosity. **Absorbency** is the ability of liquid to penetrate and be distributed through a material. It specifically relates to the wicking action of a dry clay surface when in contact with water. **Porosity** is the quantity of pores or voids in a clay body.

Wheel-Thrown Goblet
7 1/2" (19.7 cm) tall, 5" (12.7 cm) diameter
Firing: cone 10 (2,345°F [1,285°C]), soda firing
See page 161 for formula

American Society for Testing and Materials Test

This absorption testing procedure used by the ASTM is as effective as the standard test described earlier.

Equipment
- Fired clay
- Scale accurate to $\frac{1}{100}$ of a gram
- Container to boil water
- Calculator
- Damp, lint-free towel
- Metal pin stilt

Instructions

① As in the standard absorption test (see page 60), create fired test bars. Weigh the bars and record the measurements.

② Place the bars in boiling water for 5 hours. Then turn off the heat, and let the bars soak for 24 hours.

③ Remove the bars from water and carefully wipe all sides with a lint-free towel. Be sure to remove excess moisture from every facet of the clay bar, without wicking any moisture from the bars' surfaces.

④ Immediately weigh the bars.

⑤ Calculate absorption using this formula:

(saturated weight – dry weight)/dry weight x 100 = percent absorption

The absorption test bars should be smooth on each of their six sides. An indentation or void in the surface can trap water, which will alter the test results.

The Pinch Pot Absorption Test

In addition to the ASTM test and standard absorption testing techniques described, you can perform a pinch pot test to determine the likelihood of water leaking from a fired clay body.

Equipment
- Fired clay

Instructions

① Make several pinch pots and place them, unglazed, throughout your kiln.

② Once pots are out of the kiln, fill them with water and allow them to stand for 24 hours on a nonabsorbent surface. If you notice moisture under the pots the next day, the clay is absorbing water and leaking.

③ Fire the pinch pots with other pottery in the kiln, and fire to the clay body's maturity.

Correcting Absorption Problems

There are several corrections to solve absorption problems, such as firing the clay to a higher temperature, firing the clay over a longer time period, or adjusting the clay body formula by increasing the amount of flux materials (feldspar). The type and amount of additional flux will depend on the firing temperature of the clay body. If you are using a commercial clay, simply purchase a different clay body. This is a safer bet than adding materials to a supplier's clay body formula. (You don't have the exact recipe, so you could do more harm than good by mixing in additives.) Many ceramic suppliers sell several clay bodies in each temperature range.

Most important, remember when buying a clay body from a ceramics supplier to test several clay bodies at one time for shrinkage, absorption, and glaze fit before committing to an individual clay body for use in functional pottery or sculpture.

These fired unglazed pinch pots containing water show the right bowl leaking over 24 hours. When performing this test, assume that if one bowl leaks and the other bowls hold water, the reason could be a different amount of heat treatment in the kiln. Because it might be difficult to fire the kiln evenly, adjust the clay body or use another clay body formula.

A bisque-fired cup (left) compared to a higher-temperature glaze-fired cup (right). Notice the increased shrinkage in the glaze-fired cup due to clay body vitrification.

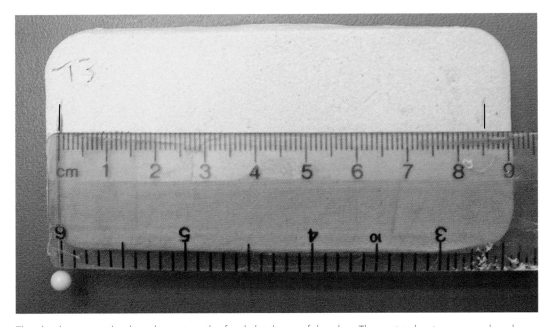

The shrinkage-test clay bar determines the fired shrinkage of the clay. The moist clay is measured and marked at 10 centimeters (not shown). After the clay bar has been fired to maturity or vitrification temperature, the clay has shrunk by 1.5 centimeters or 15 percent (8.5 cm on plastic ruler scale as measured by vertical black line drawn in clay bar).

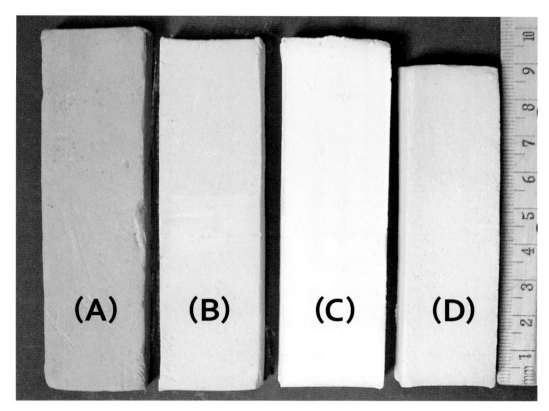

(A) Moist clay bar; (B) Bone-dry clay bar; (C) Bisque-fired clay bar; (D) Bar fired to cone 9 (2,300° F [1,260°C]) with total shrinkage rate of 12 percent.

Interpreting Absorption and Shrinkage

Both clay shrinkage and absorption cause significant changes in the ceramic form as clay dries and is eventually fired to maturity. The bars pictured here represent the same clay body in leather-hard, bone-dry, bisque-fired, and fired-to-maturity stages. With higher temperatures, increased vitrification occurs in the clay body causing greater shrinkage and lower absorption.

Bar A: Moist clay was rolled out into a slab 3.9″ (10 cm) long.

Bar B: A bone-dry bar that still contains atmospheric moisture and chemical water.

Bar C: This bisque-fired clay bar was heated to cone 06 (1,828°F [998°C]) and has an absorption rate of 14 percent. With such a high rate of absorption, it will leach water; however, it will be ideal for the absorption of a glaze application. The shrinkage rate is 7%.

Bar D: The bar was fired to cone 9 (2,300°F [1,260°C]) and has an absorption rate of 1.5 percent. Ceramic forms made from the clay fired at this temperature will hold water because of the relative nonabsorbency of the clay body. Clay bodies approaching zero-percent absorption, which can be beneficial in the translucent quality of porcelain, can develop too much glass and become brittle. The shrinkage is 12%.

Testing for Clay Shrinkage

Moist clay shrinks and loses moisture over time. Most commercially prepared clay bodies have a "storage life" of one year. Once the clay is formed into an object, the drying process continues. However, clay is only truly dried out after it has been fired in the kiln.

Firing conditions also can cause clay shrinkage. If clay is heated too fast, steam will develop, causing the clay to crack or explode in the kiln. While this violent reaction is not strong enough to damage the kiln, it can ruin adjacent pots in the kiln. Clay also shrinks as higher temperatures trigger glass formation within the clay. If the temperature increases beyond the clay body's maturity range, excessive glass formation overtakes the clay, resulting in deformation of the ware.

The shrinkage rate for a clay body is important when making wall or floor tiles, which can require exact dimensions for installation. It might also be useful to know the shrinkage rate when calculating whether functional objects—such as plates, casseroles, covered jars, and cups—can fit inside kitchen cabinets or dishwashers.

The Shrinkage Test

Here's an easy way to test for clay shrinkage.

Equipment

- Moist clay bar
- Needle tool
- Ruler

Instructions

① Start by creating 6 test bars at least 4″x 2″ x ¼″ (10.1 cm x 5.1 cm x 6 mm) You'll take the average shrink rate of these bars to get the most accurate shrinkage measurement.

② Measure 3.9″ (10 cm) from the edge of each test bar and draw a line using a needle tool. Fire the test bars in the kiln and remeasure this space (10 cm before fired). The difference indicates the clay's fired shrinkage.

③ Measure 3.9″ (10 cm) from the edge of each test bar and draw a line using a needle tool. Allow the test bars to dry naturally until they feel bone dry. Remeasure this space (10 cm before fired). The difference indicates the clay's dry shrinkage.

Thrown Cylinder by Tom White
7″ (17.8 cm) tall, 3″ (7.6 cm) diameter
Firing: Cone 9 (2300°F [1260°C]), reduction atmosphere
See page 159 for formula

TROUBLESHOOTING CLAY IMPERFECTIONS

Manufacturers' catalogues list clay's shrinkage and absorption percentages near the rated firing temperature of the clay. Percentages are best when compared with the shrinkage and absorption rates of other clays. They less accurately determine the exact shrinkage and absorption rate for the clay in your own kiln. The ceramic supplier's kiln could be fired at a slower rate of temperature increase. All of these factors cause more or less melting in the clay and a higher or lower absorption rate. Allow for a deviation of plus or minus 1 percent when testing absorption rates yourself.

Imperfections can be introduced into a clay body during the mining, processing, packing, or shipping processes. Potters have found everything from roots and stones to cigarette butts and keys in raw clay. Even in careful mixing operations, objects can find their way into clay. In general, foreign objects in clay indicate poor quality-control procedures on the supplier's end.

Imperfections can result during the mixing process (marbling and jelly roll lamination), such as variations and inconsistencies of organic materials mixed to produce a clay body formula. This chapter addresses common imperfections in premixed clay and their basic fixes.

Marbling in moist clay can occur when the raw materials are not well mixed. Depending on the raw materials used in the clay body formula, the marbling effect may be visible in the fired clay body.

Foreign Objects

Ceramics suppliers have reported gloves, bolts, feathers, rocks, nuts, roots, wood, and cigarette butts in raw clay shipped from the mine. Anything that can be found on a clay loader—jewelry, shoes, even a wallet—can crop up later in raw clay. Potters working in their studios should remove any foreign objects from their moist clay before beginning any forming operations.

Marbling

If two different clay body formulas are not separated during the mixing process, they can combine during any stage of the process and cause a marbled effect in the moist clay. Marbling can also occur when a clay body is not allowed to mix sufficiently in the clay mixer, producing an inconsistent batch of moist clay.

When clay is extruded through the pug mill (mixer), fragments of the clay body previously passed through the mill can enter the current clay mix. If the preceeding clay is the same temperature range, a discoloration is evident when the clay is at its maturing range. If the preceeding clay happens to be a lower- or higher-temperature clay, the contamination can result in a fired clay with fluxed (melted) or overly refractory (cracked) areas. Finally, if one of the clays mixed in the clay body formula has a higher level of organic material, this inconsistency will show up in the form of marbling.

Jelly Roll Lamination

Under certain pug mill conditions, the resulting mixed clay can exhibit a circular series of fault lines. The concentric shear lines look like a cross-section of a jelly roll cake. The defect is produced by the auger blades in the pug mill that create a rubbing action, separating the coarse and fine particles in a clay mix. The auger's rubbing action causes an effect similar to troweling the top layer of wet cement so fine particles migrate to the surface. Bend a thin slice of clay, and you'll see the concentric ring pattern. The defect occurs because of the combination of particle sizes in a clay body and the speed with which clay moves through the de-airing chamber of the pug mill.

One way to prevent jelly rolls is to slow the auger and thus clay movement through the chamber. Some clay bodies can tolerate fast speeds through the chamber, but others cannot. Ultimately, the side effect potters experience

Here, a low-temperature red clay is mixed with a high temperature stoneware clay. This combination can cause discoloration in the fired clay and significant fluxing action when the clay mixture is fired to high temperature.

because of jelly roll lamination is uneven particle distribution, which results in cracking in the drying, bisque-firing, or glaze-firing stages.

Always wedge clay before forming to equalize the moisture content of the clay, and thoroughly mix any shear lines created by the extrusion process, which will prevent a jelly roll lamination crack in the drying or firing stages.

Contaminated Grog

Grog is added to moist clay bodies to increase the "tooth," or stand-up ability of the clay in the throwing or hand building process. Grog also reduces the rate of dry and fired shrinkage and can add texture to the clay body surface.

Grog can either be mined as a virgin material, which contains high amounts of alumina and silica, or it can be crushed from reprocessed firebricks. Depending on the firebricks' original use, the grog can include contaminants that cause green specking in the fired clay body. While this is rare, it is always best to use virgin grog in the clay body.

The particle-size distribution of grog can shift, depending on the care with which it is processed. Coarser grog will make moist clay feel gritty, and large particles of grog may disrupt the surface texture of the clay. Finer grog particles can make the moist clay feel gummy and lacking "tooth."

A jelly roll lamination is revealed in the extruded clay. Always wedge clay before forming it to disperse uneven particles.

Raw and Fired Clay Color Differentiation

Individual materials used in the clay body formula can determine its moist color but not always its eventual fired color. The raw color of a clay body can differ considerably from its fired color, depending on the organic materials and sulfates found in any of the clays or raw materials. Metallic coloring oxides found in clays, such as iron and manganese, also can influence raw and fired color.

Firing a clay body will drive off organic materials and sulfates. Clays high in organic content can appear almost black and, with the correct firing procedure, fire out to a bright white. Raw fireclays range from light gray to brown, depending on their organic and sulfate levels. Raw ball clays, depending on their lignite content, range from cream to gray. High sulfate levels in ball clays can give them a yellow cast.

A raw material left out or added (a mixing error) in an extra quantity could change the raw color of the moist clay and the clay body's handling and firing characteristics. If a refractory fireclay component was left out of the formula, the clay body might become extremely plastic and gummy, causing it to slump or melt in the firing stages. If dark iron-bearing clays were mistakenly used in the clay body, it would be revealed in white or porcelain clays only after they have been fired.

If your moist clay is colored differently than usual, be sure to create test bars and fire the moist clay, to see if the fired color is correct.

Lamination patterns in a clay extrusion.

Opposite: Wheel-Thrown Raku-Fired Vase, by Steven Branfman
8" (20.3 cm) tall, 7" (17.8 cm) diameter
Firing: cone 04 (1,945°F [1,063°C]), fired in an oxidation atmosphere and fast-cooled in a reduction atmosphere
See page 162 for formula

Spotlight on Lime Pop

Lime pop occurs when moisture in the air comes into contact with a carbonized lime nodule, causing its expansion in an unyielding fired clay body. This can occur when the pottery is removed from the kiln. It can also happen years later, as lime expands (in the form of calcium hydroxide). Lime pop is a semi-elliptical 1/8- to 1/2-inch (3- to 13-mm) crack in low-temperature bisque or high-temperature fired ware. A conical hole reveals a black or white nodule (lime) at the bottom. .

If lime is present in the clay body as a powder, the forces of expansion are not sufficient to crack the clay. In low-fire white clay bodies, powdered limestone (composed of more than 80 percent calcium or magnesium carbonate) is often added to prevent glaze crazing (see page 112).

When used in earthenware glazes, large percentages of lime can cause crystal growth. In high-temperature glazes, limestone in powder form acts as a flux, causing other glaze materials to melt.

Limestone contamination in moist clay comes most frequently from plaster wedging tables or plaster bats. Soft or brittle plaster nodules of greater than 1/2 mm can enter the clay body during wedging or the reprocessing of scrap clay. Eventually, plaster will degrade, causing the moist clay to grab particles from the weakened plaster surface. To counter this type of mishap, staple a canvas cloth on top of the plaster wedging board and inspect plaster bats for any soft spots or concave areas.

Lime Pop Diagrams

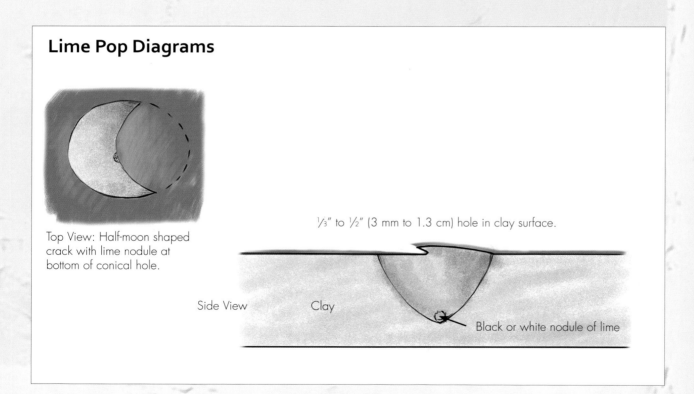

Top View: Half-moon shaped crack with lime nodule at bottom of conical hole.

1/3" to 1/2" (3 mm to 1.3 cm) hole in clay surface.

Side View   Clay

Black or white nodule of lime

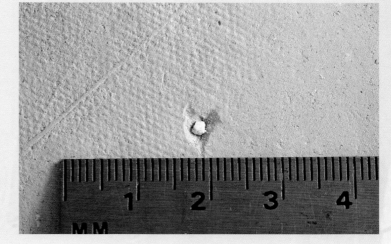

A white lime nodule at the bottom of a conical hole in the bisque-fired clay body. Note any white specks in dry or moist clay, which can be an indication of limestone particles. If only a few hard white nodules are found in the clay, simply remove them to prevent a potential lime pop.

This cross-section of a fired clay body shows voids that contain a white particle of limestone.

3

Glazes

GLAZE CHEMISTRY

Defined in the simplest terms, glaze is liquid glass subjected to heat. When glazes are fired in a kiln, they melt and adhere to the clay body, eventually hardening and forming a glossy, satin matte, or matte surface texture. Glazes contain silica, alumina, and any combination of flux oxides. Various raw materials—calcium, magnesium, frits, boron, and a multitude of others—are combined to form glazes that act differently, depending on the clay body and firing conditions. Ultimately, you will choose a glaze based on the purpose of your clay piece and your kiln's firing temperature and atmosphere.

Glazes can serve many functions. Base glazes appear transparent, semiopaque, or opaque when fired. As the name implies, these glazes often serve as a "base" for adding other materials, such as metallic coloring oxides, stains, gums, or suspension agents that alter the fired outcome. Liner glazes are applied to functional pottery, such as mugs or plates—anything you plan to use that will come into direct contact with food or drink. Liner glazes are inert when in contact with acidic or alkaline food or liquids. These glazes are durable enough to withstand dishwashing soaps—even dishwashers. Liner glazes do not contain lead or soluble materials that could leach into food or beverages, but can contain coloring oxides or stains.

The way glaze melts onto clay is like magic, or so it seems. You apply a milky white liquid to a pot, fire it in a kiln, and the final product is a rich, cobalt blue. As with many things in pottery, what you see when glaze is in its raw, pre-fired form is not what you get once the clay piece has been heated in the kiln.

Wheel-Thrown Covered Jar, by Tom White
5$\frac{1}{2}$" (14 cm) tall, 5$\frac{1}{2}$" (14.6 cm) diameter
Firing: cone 11 (2,361°F [1,294°C]) reduction
atmosphere (soda firing)
See page 160 for formula

Desirable Glaze

Reliable, defect-free glazes share certain characteristics. They apply easily onto the clay surface, whether sprayed, dipped, or brushed. Glazes that require minimum touch-ups after dipping save the studio potter time, especially if production and sales are considerations. Also, quality glazes have a temperature buffer in the kiln; preferably a two to three pyrometric cone maturing range. At either cone range, the fired pot should have a smooth, non-pitted surface. An abrasion-resistant surface is important for functional pottery. Functional pottery glazes should not leach when in contact with acidic or alkaline foods. And, most important, the best glaze formulas are reliable and yield consistent texture and color time after time.

Achieving such desirable glaze characteristics is only possible with raw materials that are reliable and stable in particle size, chemical composition, and organic content. You should examine a glaze's solubility, stability, and firing conditions to ensure the best results.

Solubility

Soluble materials will leach into the water system of the glaze, changing its chemical composition over time, which can result in multiple glaze defects. As water evaporates from the glaze layer during application, soluble materials travel by wicking action, drawing higher concentrations of material to the ridges and edges of the pot. Essentially, the glaze formula in the elevated edges of the pot is different, due to the concentration of soluble materials. The altered glaze area can cause blisters, pinholes, dry surfaces, or changes in the glaze color.

When soluble materials are required in a glaze formula, store them in waterproof plastic bags. A conservative approach is to mix only enough glaze containing soluble material for one glazing session. Remember, the stored liquid glaze can change over time.

Soluble materials include boric acid, Gerstley borate, colemanite, soda ash, wood ash, Gillespie borate, Boraq, potassium bichromate, and pearl ash (potassium carbonate). Other glaze materials, such as lithium carbonate, magnesium carbonate, nepheline syenite, strontium carbonate, and some frits, can have lesser degrees of solubility. These soluble materials can be found in glaze formulas, and they generally do not interfere with the glaze application or fired glaze effects.

Stability

When glazing pottery that you plan to use for food or liquids, you must know how the glaze will react in acidic and alkali conditions. Acidic or alkali conditions from lemons or dishwasher soap can attack glaze surfaces, resulting in discoloration, pitting, or penetration of liquids into the glaze. Extracted elements from the glaze can contaminate food or liquids.

In the presences of strong alkali (high pH) silica, the glaze converts to caustic sodium silicate, altering the original glaze as well as feeding on itself and causing further damage. In extremely acidic (low pH) conditions found in food or drink, alkalis are drawn out of unstable glazes. The leaching effect can discolor or mar the glaze surface. This reaction is often observed when tomatoes, limes, or lemon juice (all acidic) are left on compromised glazed surfaces for any length of time.

Any concave or convex disruption of the glazed surface, such as blisters, pinholes, or clay body eruptions through the glaze, are possible sources of entry for contaminants and/or corrosive reactions. Glaze defects such as crazing (see page 112), which is a fine network of recessed lines, can provide a place for bacteria and mold to grow and contaminate food or drink.

Liner Glaze Requirements

While potters have a good idea of what characteristics constitute a glaze—color, light transmission, temperature range, and surface texture—liner glazes can offer some challenges to achieve their intended function. Here are a few things to keep in mind.

- Liner glazes should not contain lead or lead frits. Although such glazes can be formulated for safe use, many variables make the formulation process and storage of raw materials impractical for most pottery operations.

- Test for solubility if the glaze contains more than 5 percent of metallic coloring oxides or stains. Metallic coloring oxides or their carbonate forms, such as cobalt oxide, cobalt carbonate, and iron oxide (which are readily soluble in the glazes) can also be used in small amounts, less than 3 percent.

- Glazed surfaces should be smooth, without concave or convex irregularities.

- Glazes should be free of crazing, a fine network of cracks in the glaze surface, and shivering, when the glaze peels off the fired clay surface similar to paint chipping.

- Glazes should apply evenly to the pottery surface by dipping, brushing, or spraying.

- Glazes should have high abrasion resistance when fired, creating a strong blemish-free surface when in contact with household utensils.

- Glazes should resist high alkali and acidic conditions in daily use.

- Glazes should be easily reproducible, giving consistent results in every kiln firing.

- Glazes should be stable when fired slightly above or below their recommended firing temperature because not all kilns will fire evenly.

- Field-test glazes in actual heating, freezing, and cleaning conditions.

- Send suspect glazes to a testing laboratory before using the formula in your studio.

Firing Conditions

Every clay body and glaze combination will react differently to the rate of temperature increase in the kiln. As a general guideline, take at least 12 to 14 hours total firing time to reach cone 6, or 2,232°F (1,222°C), in a fully-loaded, electric kiln. In a computer-controlled electric kiln, use the "slow" setting with a fully-loaded kiln. (For more information on kiln temperature, see page 86.)

If there are not enough pots to fill the kiln, place shelves and posts in the kiln to create greater thermal mass, which will contribute to an even heat distribution and slow the rate of heating and cooling. Hydrocarbon-fueled kilns and/or larger kilns with greater thermal mass may require different firing cycles to achieve glaze and clay body maturity.

Glaze maturity is especially important in liner glazes, because they are often applied to enclosed forms, such as covered jars, teapots, or casseroles, which can be insulated somewhat from outside heat sources. Ceramic materials are good insulators of heat, and an enclosed interior glaze surface will not mature like the outside glazed surface if the kiln is fired too fast or does not reach glaze maturing temperature. Determine kiln temperature by placing pyrometric cones inside the kiln, or by taking a pyrometer reading.

Firing the glaze too fast to its end-point temperature can result in microscopic, rough, and jagged surfaces. Kiln firing conditions can change the glaze surface and clay body maturity, causing it to leach its oxides or trap food particles. Also, glazes and clay bodies can become unstable in over-reduced or under-reduced kiln atmospheres, or when exposed to wood, salt, or soda firing. Atmospheric kiln firing conditions can introduce variable factors that slow or intensify the melting action and surface texture of the glaze formula.

In other instances, the clay body itself can alter the glaze by drawing out oxides from the glaze. This will inhibit the glaze's melting potential, resulting in a surface that leaches water or an unsanitary surface that traps food particles in its microscopic voids (due to glaze not melting completely). Some matte glazes can be unstable, leaching their oxides into foods or liquids because they achieve their matte effect through under-firing or fast firing. Such glazes also can cause chipping, crazing, and scratching, or display a bleached lighter fired color.

TIP

Using Trial and Error

Test kilns allow the trial and error adjustments of several different glaze formulas. If successful, glazes can be produced in larger amounts for pottery production.

Testing Glaze

Always test glazes before applying them to pottery. Glazes will react differently on brown and white clays and when subjected to different firing temperatures. Because you are not using the same kiln as the ceramics supplier, do not rely on their test tile samples as a completely accurate depiction of how a glaze will look after it is fired.

Equipment

100-gram test batch of glaze

80-mesh sieve

4″ (10-cm) test tiles, with smooth and textured surfaces

Bucket

Instructions

1. Measure out a 100-gram test batch of glaze (dry material).

2. Add enough water to achieve a glaze thickness of 0.5 mm to 1.5 mm or the equivalent of 3 business cards stacked together.

3. Strain the mixture through an 80-mesh sieve, allowing the glaze to collect in a bucket.

4. Apply the glaze to several 4″ test tiles with smooth and textured surfaces. Allow for a 1″ unglazed area on the bottom of each tile, because some glazes might drip.

5. Place the test tiles on the top, middle, and bottom shelves of the kiln. Not all kilns fire evenly, so this will give an indication of how the kiln's heat work affects the glaze. The multiple tiles will indicate the temperature range at which the glaze will mature.

If the kiln were firing to a higher temperature, on the top, the glaze might have an exceptionally high glossy surface and run on the vertical tile. If in another part of the kiln the temperature was too low, the same glaze might have a dry matte surface and not run on the vertical tile. If the same glaze looks identical despite variations in temperature throughout the kiln, it is an indication of an adequate glaze maturation range.

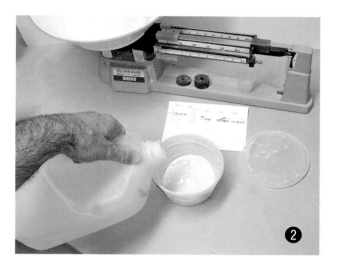

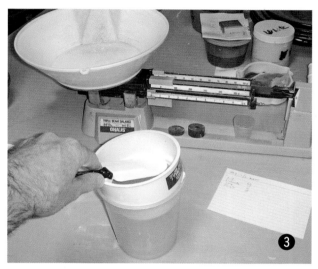

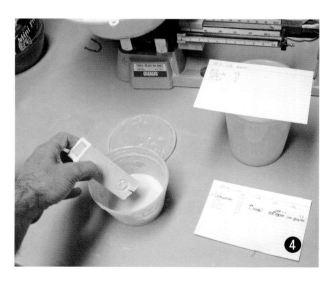

Glazes for Foods and Beverages

Many potters will use a glaze habitually without considering how it will react when coming into contact with food or drink. Some potters believe any glaze that melts can serve as a liner glaze. However, not every liner glaze can stand up to alkaline/acidic conditions or produce an abrasion-resistant surface.

The three factors that influence more than 90 percent of attack by acidic and alkali substances on unstable glazes are time, temperature, and extreme pH levels. The remaining 10 percent encompasses the hardness of the water, sanitary condition of the container, and any suspended material in the water. The longer a glaze is exposed to acidic or alkali substances, the greater the chance of leaching. Additionally, the higher the temperature of acidic or alkali substances, the greater the possibility of leaching. Extremely low or high pH levels can increase leaching in glazes. It's important to note that with normal pottery use, time, temperature, and pH conditions will have no adverse effect on *stable* glazes, only unstable glazes.

Acid/Alkaline Resistance

Several selections of raw glaze materials can enhance glaze stability in acidic and alkali conditions. Acidic conditions attack alkaline materials in the glaze such as feldspars or high-alkaline frits. To a lesser degree, they also react with alkaline earth materials in the glaze, such as dolomite, calcium carbonate, or magnesium carbonate and strontium carbonate.

Often, decreasing a glaze's alkaline-earth oxides (such as barium oxide, calcium oxide, or magnesium oxide) and substituting alkaline oxides (such as sodium oxide, potassium oxide, lead oxide, lithium oxide, or titanium oxide) will increase its resistance to acid/alkaline conditions. However, high percentages of a single alkaline-earth material can contribute to a matte surface texture and glaze instability. Alkaline-earth oxides can be found in several ceramic materials, such as barium carbonate, whiting, magnesium carbonate, dolomite, and talc. Alkaline oxides can be found in several ceramic materials such as feldspars, frits, lead, lithium carbonate, and titanium dioxide.

Because both groups of alkaline and alkaline-earth materials act as fluxes in varying strengths, they should be used in the lowest amounts possible to achieve a glassy melt. Alkaline and alkaline-earth fluxes will not contribute color to glazes, but they do influence color when metallic coloring oxides are present in the glaze. Greater glaze stability can be achieved by using combinations of fluxes, as opposed to a single flux.

Increasing the silica content of a glaze can prevent acidic and alkali reactions on the glaze surface. However, a glaze with not enough flux and too high a silica content will be immature and subject to chemical attack, while additions of alumina, titania, and zirconia improve a glaze's acid resistance. A common source of titania is titanium dioxide. Superpax, Opax, and Ultrox (or their equivalents) are glaze opacity–producing agents that contain zirconia. A balance of fluxes, alumina, and silica will produce stable glazes along with the appropriate firing conditions.

A surprising number of glazes, when critically examined, are overly fluxed and can accept more silica (flint) to achieve a resilient glaze. One indication of overly fluxed glazes is running on vertical surfaces or even a slight beading on the bottom of the form where the glaze ends and the foot begins.

Some glazes are "soft" when fired, meaning they can be easily abraded by utensil marks in daily use. Glaze designed for functional pottery must meet the test of abrasion resistance.

Abrasion Resistance

When a glaze shows scratch marks, the physically soft quality of the glaze is giving way to a harder material moving across the surface. Some glazes are soft compared with household utensils and scrubbing pads. Glazes can be scratched when they have not reached their maturation temperature or if they reached their correct temperature too quickly. Both conditions can result in insufficient glass formation in the glaze. Often, immature glazes are incorrectly classified as satin matte or matte, with a semi-opaque or opaque light transmission and a rough surface texture.

The simplest solution is to fire the glaze to a higher temperature and/or longer time to temperature, which will result in glaze maturity. Both firing methods subject the glaze to greater heat work in the kiln. This causes silica and alumina contained in the glaze formula to reach a glassy hard consistency. Or, try increasing the primary glaze fluxes, such as feldspars or frits. (Remember, adding too much feldspar or frit can subject the glaze to acidic or alkali attack.) A careful balance of flux materials, silica, and alumina fired to maturity in a compatible kiln firing cycle will develop glazes that resist chemical attack and abrasion.

Using Metallic Coloring Oxides

Do not overload a durable, safe glaze with metallic coloring oxides, such as cobalt, copper, or chrome. When multiple metallic oxides are used, even in low levels, their combined effect can cause leaching in a stable base glaze. The amount of oxides it takes to overload a base glaze depends on the base glaze formula, firing temperature, time to temperature, kiln atmosphere, glaze application thickness, and clay body composition.

Liner glazes should have a smooth surface that can contain food or liquid in an inert condition. The fired glaze should be easy to clean and not subject to alkaline or acid attack. Below, a stoneware bowl, 12" (30 cm) in diameter.

ADJUSTING AND TESTING GLAZES

At some point, you will want to experiment with glazes. Whether using commercial premixed glazes or your own formulas, venturing outside of the familiar into new glaze palettes is important. Before you do so, understand how raw materials, particle size, kiln atmosphere, and other variables affect a glaze formula.

This pitcher was dipped in ZAM Gloss Blue cone 9 glaze.

Ask the Right Questions

Each ceramics supplier can use different sources for the raw materials they sell to potters. To further complicate things, generic names are often used for raw materials that are often not an accurate representation of specific materials. Also, each processor or wholesaler of raw material can have several different grades of that material. The result is a common name for a raw material that can be completely different depending on where it is processed and eventually sold.

Nevertheless, the largest areas of misunderstanding occur when potters do not fully appreciate the effects of heat work on clay and glazes. Every kiln heats and cools differently. Sometimes, the difference is enough to change a glaze radically. When a glaze formula states it should be fired to cone 9 (2,300°F [1,260°C]), do you know what size kiln the glaze was fired in or how long it took to reach the glaze maturing temperature?

Following is a sample of a typical glaze formula and questions you should ask a ceramics supplier concerning the raw materials it contains. These questions address particle size, chemical composition, solubility, and the existence of additives such as metallic coloring oxide.

Glaze Contents	Questions
ZAM Gloss Blue c/9	What is the kiln firing atmosphere?
Nepheline syenite 55	What mesh size?
Flint 27	What mesh size?
Whiting 8	What is the chemical composition and particle size?
Gerstley borate 10	Is this variable in chemical composition, and is it soluble?
Cobalt oxide 6%	What is the strength of the metallic coloring oxide?

A functional piece is dipped into a bucket of glaze. Stir the glaze periodically during glazing operations to prevent it from settling in the bucket. Each glaze might require a shorter or longer interval between stirring due to the density of its raw materials.

TIP

Ceramic raw materials are processed in different mesh sizes. The higher the mesh number, the smaller the particle size. For example, flint can be obtained in 60x—a granular particle, 200x—a powder, or finer grades up to and exceeding 440x.

Particle Size

The particle sizes of ceramic raw materials are critical factors in their ability to melt. A smaller particle size denotes increased surface area, which melts more efficiently than a larger particle size. A finer mesh material might cause a lower melting point, which can result in the fired glaze dripping or a semi-opaque glaze appearing transparent. All glaze materials look like powder, so knowing the actual mesh size is important for duplicating any glaze formula. For example, flint, a glass-forming oxide and major component in any glaze, can be purchased in 60x mesh, 100x mesh, 200x mesh, 325x mesh, and 400x mesh. (Larger numbers indicate finer particles.) Even finer mesh sizes are available by special order. Frequently, a glaze formula will not specify a mesh size for flint. In such instances, use 325x mesh flint.

When you screen glaze material in your own studio, reach for the 80x mesh sieve. The small size of the screen causes a mechanical mixing action of the glaze materials suspended in the glaze water. The sieve breaks down any nodules or conglomerate particles into a homogenized mixture of material and water. A coarser open-mesh sieve can allow large particles of material such as kaolin or flint to mix into the glaze and appear as small specks on the glazed surface. The screening process is especially important for soluble materials, such as Gerstley borate, colemanite, soda ash, borax, or pearl ash (potassium carbonate). These can clump together in storage and must be broken into smaller particles.

It's important to note that metallic coloring oxides and their reaction with glazes can also be influenced by the size of the screen. For example, cobalt oxide, when used in a satin matte or matte glaze, can sometimes reveal itself as a blue glaze with blue specks in the fired glaze surface. The larger particle size of cobalt oxide as compared to cobalt carbonate will pass through undisturbed in a coarser mesh sieve.

Testing glazes can offer the potter an assurance of a good result. Pottery is time- and labor-intensive, and it can be discouraging to unload a kiln with glaze defects. Always test any glaze before committing yourself to a large body of work.

Kiln Size and Atmosphere

When selecting a glaze, keep in mind how that glaze will be affected by your kiln's size, atmosphere, and firing cycle. As a general guideline, the chart below illustrates what happens to a clear, transparent glaze when subjected to a cone 6 (2,232°F [1,222°C]) firing in small, medium, and large kiln electric kilns. The time to cone 6 was approximately the same in each kiln firing, with the only difference being kiln size. The larger kilns, having more thermal mass, created more "heat work" in the kiln with greater glaze maturation, resulting in a smooth, transparent glaze with a hard durable surface. The craze lines produced by the 1-cubic-foot kiln were due to the immaturity of the clay body with the glaze under tension upon cooling.

The size of the kiln can play an important part in the development of surface texture (gloss, satin matte, dry matte), light transmission (clear, semi-opaque, opaque), color (red, green, blue, brown etc.) and glaze hardness (soft surface, easily scratched or hard surface-abrasion resistant). Ceramic materials melt under several conditions aside from the absolute, or end-point temperature, they reach in the kiln. The time it takes to reach that temperature and the rate of cooling are factors that inhibit or promote more melting in clay bodies and glazes.

Kiln size also influences the vitreous quality of the clay body. Larger kilns have greater thermal mass. Kiln bricks, posts, shelves, and stacked pots are all factors that radiate heat. Larger kilns radiate more heat during their heating and cooling cycles than smaller kilns. The larger kiln promotes more heat work and greater melting in clay bodies and glazes. Larger kilns can cause a different glaze reaction compared to smaller kilns with less thermal mass, which dissipate heat at a faster rate. Because small test kilns have less thermal mass, they are an inaccurate indicator of clay body and glaze reactions if you will use a larger kiln in production.

Kiln Firing Cycle

Do you know the kiln firing cycle of the glaze? If so, there is a greater chance of duplicating the glaze. A fast-kiln firing cycle will produce an immature clay body that can be highly absorbent, less durable, and contribute to glaze problems such as crazing. A fast-kiln firing cycle can alter the fired color, texture, glaze durability, and light transmission of the glaze, while an excessively long firing cycle can cause the glaze to become markedly glossy or to run off vertical surfaces. Some glazes work best when held at their maturing temperature for a given period of time. Other glazes, when held at temperature, can blister or run down vertical surfaces due to increased heat work on the glaze at the high end of glaze vitrification. The kiln cooling cycle also can play an important part in the development of a glaze. Devitrification or crystal growth can cause small or large crystals to develop in the cooling glaze. The growth of crystals is dependent, in part, on the glaze formula, clay body, and rate of cooling.

While there are no perfect kiln firing cycles that will work for every glaze, a 75°F to 80°F (24°C to 26°C) heat increase per hour from cone 6 (2,232 °F [1,222°C]) to cone 9 (2,300°F [1,260°C]) using self-supporting Orton cones is a recommended starting point for high-temperature cone 9 glazes.

Do you know what kind of atmosphere was used in the glaze firing? Electric kilns generate clean oxidation atmospheres. However, carbon-based fuels such as natural gas, propane, wood, coal, oil, and sawdust can produce oxidation, neutral, and reduction atmospheres. **Oxidation** is when there is more oxygen than fuel in the combustion process. **Neutral** occurs when there are equal amounts of oxygen and fuel in the combustion process. **Reduction** atmospheres have more fuel than oxygen in the combustion process. Reduction kiln atmospheres can cause greater melting, due to the increased fluxing action of the metallic coloring oxides contained in the clay body and glaze. Variations in the duration and amount of reduction can also change clay body and glaze colors and glaze surface textures. The variability of the reduction kiln firing atmosphere is usually responsible for glazes not firing as expected.

Kiln Size as a Determinant of Fired Glaze Characteristics

Size of Kiln	Surface texture	Light transmission	Glaze hardness
Small: 1 cu/ft.	dry rough	opaque/crazed lines	easily scratched
Medium: 5 cu/ft.	slightly rough	semi-opaque	hard
Large: 12 cu/ft.	smooth	transparent	hard

Kiln atmosphere can affect any glaze color, texture, or melting capacity. For instance, the cobalt oxide in ZAM Gloss Blue will fire blue in almost any kiln atmosphere, but its color intensity will vary, depending on the atmosphere in the kiln and fuel used to maintain that atmosphere. In soda and salt firings, ZAM Gloss Blue can run or drip on vertical surfaces or pool in horizontal areas, due to the fluxing action of sodium vapor in the kiln atmosphere. In wood-fired kilns, the alkaline content of the wood ash during the firing can flux the glaze excessively, causing glaze dripping and glossy areas. In many instances, the glaze reactions to salt and wood firing are aesthetically positive. But both atmospheres can flux or melt the pyrometric cones prematurely if they are not protected.

Do you know the exact position of the cone in the glaze firing? Potters read the melting of pyrometric cones at different positions. Some potters consider the cone at its correct temperature when it bends at the 3 o'clock or 9 o'clock position (or, bending over half way in relation to the bottom of the cone pack). Other potters read the cone as being down when it actually touches the cone pack. Certain glazes are very sensitive to slight temperature variations indicated by the exact position of the pyrometric cone. In these glazes, the exact position of the cone can alter color, opacity, or glaze texture.

Keep in mind kilns can "coast," or continue to supply more heat work to the clay body and glaze after the kiln has been shut down. This condition can be observed when the potter turns off the kiln and notices that the position of the cone has fallen as the kiln cools.

Raw Material Substitutions

Many glaze formulas were first developed using feldspars, clays, or other raw materials that are no longer in production. Even if the raw material is still in production, it might have subtly changed in chemical composition, particle size, or organic content, all of which can alter the current glaze result.

The best course of action, though time-consuming and somewhat inefficient, is to test raw materials before committing to a large production batch of glaze. You should also ask the ceramics supplier if there have been any current problems or customer complaints with a raw material. Apply the same "always changing" mentality for clay with glaze materials.

If a substitution is required, clays in the glaze formula should be replaced within the same general group, such as ball clays, kaolins, or fireclays. Each group has subgroups based on metallic oxide content, plasticity, organic content, and particle-size distribution. However, a good starting point is to obtain a chemical analysis sheet from the ceramics supplier. The information listed will determine the most suitable substitution.

Typical cone pack configuration for a kiln being fired to cone 6 (2,232°F [1,222°C], second cone from left.)

TIP

Studio Note

Test-fire different glazes in close proximity to find out how they will react in the same kiln.

Fuming occurs when part of the glaze formula vaporizes during the firing. A fuming reaction is most noticeable when a glaze containing chrome oxide is placed next to a glaze containing tin oxide. A pink blush on the glaze containing tin is the result.

Metallic Coloring Oxide/ Carbonates

Use the same processor of metallic coloring oxides when ordering materials. If this is not possible, test the oxide. Metallic coloring oxides and their carbonate forms are processed by different international companies. Oxides include cobalt oxide, cobalt carbonate, manganese dioxide, manganese carbonate, copper oxide, copper carbonate, nickel oxide, and nickel carbonate, along with chrome oxide, iron chromate, rutile light, rutile dark, llmenite powder, red iron oxide and its variations. Each can differ in purity, particle size, and trace material content, depending on the processing plant. For example, cobalt oxide (Co_3O_4) is processed in three grades: 71.5 percent, 72.5 percent ceramic grade, and 73.5 percent. The percentage represents the cobalt contained in the oxide. Each grade can affect the intensity of the blue that will be generated in a glaze.

In addition, the quantity of trace elements in a metallic coloring oxide can influence its effect on the glaze color. Although slight differences in trace metallic oxide content usually will not cause a radical color change, particle size can affect the look of a glaze. A coarser particle size of cobalt oxide can cause blue specks in a glaze; a finer grind of the same oxide (or cobalt carbonate, which is a finer grind) will just produce a blue color glaze field.

Glaze Water and Soluble Materials

The amount of water used in a glaze formula is rarely stated. The volume of water added to a dry glaze is one of the major areas of miscalculation, and that can result in too thin or too thick of a glaze layer on the ceramic ware. Each formula requires a specific amount of water, due to the particle density of the raw materials, glaze suspension additives, glaze gums, glaze material solubility, and the chemical composition of the water used in mixing the glaze. The method of application—sprayed, dipped, or brushed—also affects the water needed for success.

Water quality can affect the glaze viscosity (thickness or thinness). The hardness of the water can cause the glaze to flocculate (liquid glaze appears thick in the bucket), and soft water can deflocculate (liquid glaze appears thin in the bucket). Soluble glaze materials can break down in the water system of the glaze, depending on the chemical composition of the water and the level of soluble materials in the glaze. Excess water poured from a glaze can alter the chemical composition of the glaze, since soluble material may have dissolved in the water.

Dry soluble materials can also take on moisture in storage. Soluble material weight can change, depending on the amount of moisture it has absorbed, with such transformations having an effect on the total glaze formula.

Notice the fuming reaction on this test tile. A metallic salt (stannous chloride) is introduced into the kiln while it is still hot, leaving a colorful film on the previously fired glaze surface.

Pottery fired in an oxidation kiln atmosphere, which can produce consistent clay body and glaze colors.

Vitreous Qualities

When testing a glaze formula, consider the vitreous characteristics of the clay body.

The clay body and glaze interface is where fired clay and glaze meet and fuse together in the ceramic structure. The interface plays an important part in the development of the fired glaze. The interaction of clay body and glaze can influence the texture of the glaze, depending on the clay body formula, glaze formula, kiln atmosphere, and clay body maturity. Some clay bodies will draw part of the flux content from the forming glaze during the firing process. This reaction can cause opacity in light transmission or dry surface textures in the glaze.

Examples of opaque, semi-opaque, and transparent glazes.

Adjusting Clay Content

While any glaze can be altered by several methods, a simple technique is to manipulate its clay component. You do not have to know how every possible raw material reacts in a glaze, but it's a good idea to study ten to twelve of the most commonly used raw materials. Clay is a component in a large percentage of glazes.

Even if clay is not part of the original formula, you can add it to glaze as a suspension agent. Added clay will stop a glaze from dripping or will create matte, opaque surfaces.

However, note that clay additions will also increase the glaze opacity and cause a rough surface texture, depending on the amount of clay introduced into the formula.

On the other hand, removing the clay component from glaze creates a more fluid mixture with less opacity. Remove clay from a glaze mixture in 5- to 10-part increments.

Transparent to Opaque-Matte Glazes: Modifying Clay Content

The clay component of this glaze is called E.P.K. (Edgar Plastic Kaolin), a plastic, high-temperature kaolin. Increasing the E.P.K. component of a transparent, glossy glaze by 15 parts and 30 parts, based on the dry weight of the glaze, causes it to become opaque and matte.

Transparent Gloss Glaze (original glaze formula)	Parts
Nepheline Syenite 270x	20
Whiting	20
E.P.K.	20
Flint 325x	20
Ferro frit #3124	20

Matte Glaze (addition of 30 parts of E.P.K.)	Parts
Nepheline syenite 270x	20
Whiting	20
E.P.K.	50
Flint 325	20
Ferro frit #3124	20

Semi-opaque Satin (addition of 15 parts of E.P.K.)	Parts
Nepheline Syenite 270x	20
Whiting	20
E.P.K.	35
Flint 325x	20
Ferro frit #3124	20

Creating Test Tiles

Occasionally, a glaze formula will not work as expected. Start by mixing a small batch of glaze; the main goal when testing glazes is to find out how they react on a small scale. If the tests are not successful, you have a chance to adjust the glaze for further testing before mixing a large volume.

When you test, keep a notebook at hand so you can write down each weigh-out of material. Record all tests in your notebook. In a very short time, the number of test pieces can grow. A notation system allows you to refer to past glaze test results without guesswork. You'll avoid making the same mistakes twice.

Preparing Tiles

Vertical test tiles should be at least 4″ (10 cm) in height and 2″ (5 cm) wide. Test tiles must also be of sufficient surface area to approximate the actual pottery. Many times, a small test tile will be successful because the molten weight of the glaze is not heavy enough to cause it to run down vertical surfaces. However, when larger areas are glazed, the weight of the fluid glaze might cause it to be pulled down, causing drips or runs on the pots or kiln shelves. The lesson: Don't skimp on size when creating test tiles for glaze.

Place the test tiles in many kiln locations to give an indication of how well the glaze responds to different temperatures. Not every kiln fires evenly, and the test tiles will show the maturing range of the glaze. Also, the results of one glaze test should not be the determining factor indicating a successful glaze. It should be followed by placing more glaze tests in several different firings.

For accurate results, form test tiles from the same clay and technique you'll use in production. Your goal during the testing process is to obtain as much information as possible from the test tile, so you know what to expect when you apply glaze to your bisque-fired work.

Cylinders glazed in (left to right): transparent gloss, semi-opaque, and opaque matte.

TIP

Test Glaze Batch

A 300-gram batch of glaze with the appropriate amount of water should be adequate to glaze several test tiles. The tiles can then be placed in a number of different kiln firings. If the test glaze does not need an adjustment, it is often a good policy to mix up a pre-production batch of 4,000 grams, or roughly 1 liquid gallon. This larger batch will allow you to glaze several pots and place them throughout the kiln.

Preparing the Glaze Mixture

As a general guideline, approximately, 4,000 grams (141 oz) of dry glaze materials will yield 1 liquid gallon (3.8 L) of glaze. Following are steps to make 1 gallon of glaze. Not every glaze will conform to this ratio, but it is a good starting point whenever a dry raw material has to be added to a liquid glaze. Such additions can occur when adding a suspension agent, metallic coloring oxide, gum, stain, or dye to a glaze.

Equipment

- Triple beam balance scale with scoop and counterweight
- 80x mesh sieve
- Glaze bucket
- Mixing spoon
- Test tiles ready for glazing

Instructions

① Measure out 4,000 grams (141 oz) of dry glaze material.

② After the dry materials are accurately weighed, add water to the mixture. Every glaze will require different amounts, but it is best to use less water at first. You can always add more later.

③ Place the glaze mixture through an 80x mesh sieve 3 times. In most instances, a 60x mesh sieve is too coarse and will allow larger particles of raw materials to remain in the liquid glaze. A100x mesh sieve will take longer for the wet glaze to pass through. If a wet glaze is stored for a week or longer, it should be sieved again.

④ Glaze settles over time. Add 2 percent bentonite (80 grams [2.8 oz]) to ensure that the glaze mixture stays in suspension.

⑤ Bentonite will not completely blend into the liquid glaze. Therefore, sieve the entire mixture (80x mesh) three times.

Dipping Test Tiles

This procedure allows before and after comparison of how thick to apply the glaze in the next glazing session.

Equipment

- Triple beam balance scale with scoop and counterweight
- 80x mesh sieve

Wheel-Thrown/Hand-Built Sculptural Disk
11" (27.9 cm) tall, 12" (30.5 cm) diameter
Firing: cone 9 (2,300°F [1,260°C]) reduction atmosphere, unglazed
See page 157 for formula

- Glaze bucket
- Mixing spoon
- Test tiles ready for glazing
- Needle tool

Instructions

① To obtain the optimum glaze layer on test tiles, start with an application thickness of 3 cardboard matchbook covers stuck together, or slightly thinner than a dime. About 80 percent of glazes will work successfully within these parameters.

② Leave several glazed test pieces out of the firing. Compare the unfired pieces to the test pieces that went into the kiln.

③ Using a needle tool, scratch down through the unfired glaze test to the bisque surface, visually noting the glaze thickness.

Useful Glaze Tests

No two glazes will react the same on a clay body, or in your kiln, for that matter. Before you dip a prized piece into a glaze mixture, be sure the glaze has been tested. You can test-glaze for its reaction to alkaline and acid exposure, its resistance to abrasion, and ability to withstand thermal shock. (You want to know your teacup will tolerate near-boiling water.) Following are some practical tests you should execute on test tiles.

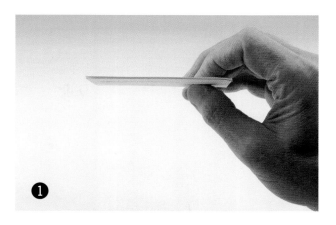

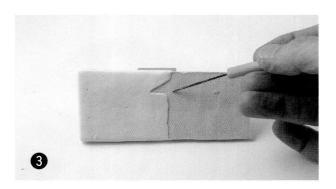

Test tiles that have been glaze fired; unfired tiles

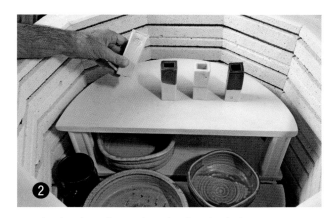

Alkali Exposure Test 1

Remember, dishwasher liquids have relatively high pH levels, which can model alkaline exposure to glazed surfaces.

Equipment

- Glazed and fired tiles
- Dishwasher
- Dishwasher detergent

Instructions

Run several glazed and fired test tiles through multiple dishwasher cycles and note color or texture differences. Reserve a control tile that has not been placed through the dishwasher for comparison.

Alkali Exposure Test 2

Baking soda (sodium carbonate) also has a relatively high pH level, which can model alkaline exposure from other sources that might come into contact with glazed surfaces.

Equipment

- Hot water
- Baking soda
- Glazed and fired tiles
- Control sample of the fired glaze

Instructions

Mixing solution: Start with hot water and slowly add baking soda (sodium carbonate) until the mixture has reached a saturation point where no more of the baking soda can be suspended in the water. Mix the solution until it is a thick soup consistency. Stir the mixture until all particles dissipate. Some potters will compare an ideal mixture thickness for application to a cross between thin cream and half-and-half.

Place the glazed tile into the solution. Withdraw the tile and allow it to sit for 24 hrs.

Rinse the glazed tile with water and wipe dry. Note any color or texture differences as compared to a control sample of the fired glaze.

Acid Exposure Test

Many foods are acidic. Often, staining can occur when acidic foods such as blueberries, tomatoes, or limes are left on an unstable glaze surface.

Alkali discoloration on glazed plate.

Equipment

- Lemon
- Glazed and fired test tile
- Control sample of the fired glaze

Instructions

① Cut the lemon in half.

② Leave the lemon, exposed surface down, on the glazed/fired test tile.

③ Wait 24 hours. Note alterations in glaze color by comparing it with the control sample of the fired glaze. If any discoloration or bleaching is evident, the glaze will not be stable in everyday use.

Abrasion-Resistance Test

Pottery that fails abrasion resistance testing might also be subject to alkali/acid attack. Plus, scratches can collect bacteria and mold, therefore contaminating food.

Equipment

- Glazed and fired test tile
- Steak knife
- Fork

Instructions

① Run a steak knife over the glazed surface, as though you are cutting food.

② Make similar movements against the test tile with the tines of a fork.

③ Continue this abrasion and observe results. Look for scratches.

Wheel-Thrown Covered Jar, 7″ (17.8 cm) tall, 8″ (20.3 cm) diameter
Firing: cone 10 (2,345°F [1,285°C]), reduction atmosphere
See page 161 for formula

THERMAL SHOCK TEST

If the clay body/glaze combinations are unstable, the pot will eventually break when in contact with boiling water. Sharp, jagged cracks can also occur when pots are taken from a refrigerator and placed in a hot oven. Both failures are due to thermal shock. Ideally, clay and glaze should cool in the kiln at a compatible rate, with the glaze staying under slight compression. If the glaze is under tension, crazing can result (a fine network of fault lines in the glaze). Shivering can occur if the glaze cools under extreme compression, causing slivers of sharp glaze sheets to break off from the underlying clay body. Unstable clay body/glaze combinations and extreme temperatures can stress the pottery's ability to remain intact. We'll discuss crazing and shivering more in a later chapter, page 106.

Perform a thermal shock test to find out how your finished pottery (fired clay and glaze) will handle extreme heat and cold.

Equipment

- Glazed and fired test pot
- Freezer
- Clean, lint-free cloth
- Water-based ink (optional)
- Metal screwdriver

Instructions

① Place the pottery in the freezer for 3 hours. Remove and carefully fill the pot with boiling water.

② Pour boiling water out of the pot and dry it with a clean, lint-free cloth.

③ Examine the pot carefully for defects. You may wish to apply a water-based ink to the surface of the pot to identify craze lines. When testing dark glazes, which can hide defects, place the pot over steam and study the surface. Caution: Always protect yourself from the boiling water and steam by wearing long oven mitts.

④ Test for shivering by tapping the side of the pot with a metal screwdriver to see if sheets of glaze begin to peel off. If so, you can assume that all glazes with the same clay body/glaze formula combination are suspect.

ASTM THERMAL SHOCK TEST

This stock test conforms to the American Society for Testing and Materials.

Equipment

- Glazed and fired pot
- Oven
- Clean, lint-free cloth

Instructions

① Place the pottery in an oven heated to 250°F (121°C) for at least 45 minutes. Remove the pottery from the oven and carefully pour room-temperature water into the form. Allow the water to cool. Dump out the water and dry out the pot, using a clean, lint-free cloth.

② Examine the pot for defects. If the pottery is still defect-free, repeat the test 3 times, increasing the oven temperature by 25°F (12°C) each time, until the final oven temperature is 325°F (162°C).

Glaze Calculation Software

Formulating new glazes or adjusting existing formulas is much easier and faster today, thanks to glaze calculation software. These programs give you the ability to add or delete materials from the glaze and observe the results on several levels, such as batch weight and unity formula. The impressive factor in calculation programs is their ability to compress the whole process of formulation, allowing the potter to obtain an overall picture of the glaze at every step of adjustment.

One of the most effective ways to use the software is in conjunction with actual glaze testing. If the fired glaze needs revising, you can quickly recalculate it with the software. One or two cycles of calculation and testing should yield a successful glaze.

When using glaze calculation programs or developing your own glaze formulas, always use the recent chemical analyses of the raw materials. Over time, raw materials such as feldspars and clays can shift in their oxide content. A ceramics supply company might not have the current chemical analysis sheets on each raw material. In such cases, contact the mine or processor for up-to-date information.

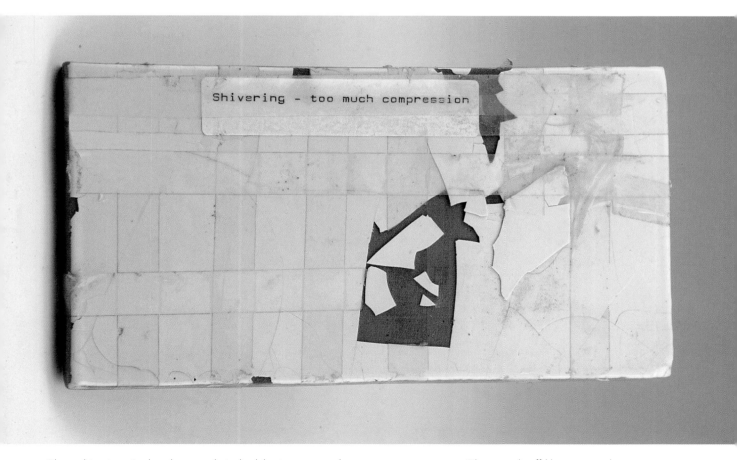

Glaze shivering. As the glaze cools in the kiln, it comes under extreme compression. Glaze peels off like a paint chip.

GLAZE TECHNIQUE

Application techniques and glaze thickness can greatly influence the final result. Each technique can deposit varying layers of glaze on edges and recessed areas of the ware, resulting in an uneven glaze coat. A stiff glaze that does not move or flow when it is melting can reveal brush strokes on the finished ware due to the bristles moving the glaze aside during the application process. Thick applications of glaze can cause glaze to flow when mature or pool and collect in recessed areas of the form. Often, glaze formulas do not include a notation on the specific techniques used to apply the glaze or the correct thickness of glaze, all of which can change how it duplicates in its fired state.

Glazes can be sprayed, dipped, or brushed. Generally, a spray application will impart a more uniform glaze layer than a dipped or brushed application. However, much depends on the skill of the individual potter as to the application technique(s), which will result in the fired glaze result. Dipping a ceramic piece into a glaze can sometimes result in drips as excess glaze runs off the ceramic surface during the initial stages of drying. A glaze drip shows most prominently in the fired ware, because this is where the glaze layer is thicker, revealing the true color and/or opacity of the glaze. Brushing the glaze can result in uneven thickness, depending on the viscosity of the glaze and the skill of the potter in the application technique. When possible, determine how thick the glaze was applied and what method of application was used, along with any special glazing techniques. Often this type of information is difficult to obtain, but as a general rule 80 percent of glazes will be functional if the glaze application equals three business cards in thickness.

Functional stoneware pottery

Technique: Dipping Glaze

Dipping a piece of pottery into glaze can impart a smooth, even application of glaze on forms such as plates, cups, bowls, or platters. However, pots that have ridges or surface protrusions can deflect the glaze, causing drips.

The glaze should be thoroughly mixed to prevent denser and heavier materials from settling to the bottom.

The plate is slowly dipped into the glaze, distributing an even coating. Larger forms require greater care, as the weight of the glaze suspended in water can cause cracking due to overstressing the bisque pottery.

Hold the plate in a vertical position to prevent the water weight contained in the glaze from cracking the bisque.

Some glazes, depending on the density of their raw materials, require frequent stirring to keep the glaze in suspension.

Technique: Spraying Glaze

Spraying imparts an even application of glaze.

Spraying can also be an effective method for applying glaze in once-firing, as the atomized glaze contains less water, allowing for a better mechanical glaze fit on the leather-hard or bone-dry clay.

The liquid glaze is poured into the spray gun container. After each spraying application, the container should be shaken to prevent the glaze from settling. Agitating the glaze will ensure a uniform glaze content in the spray.

The spray gun should be thoroughly cleaned after any spraying application.

Technique: Brushing Glaze

Brushing allows for the glaze to be applied to specific areas of the pottery. Care must be taken to ensure an even glaze coating.

1

Carefully brush the glaze on the bisque pot.

2

Clean the brush after any glaze application.

Studio Note

The depth of the glaze layer can play an important part in duplicating a glaze effect. If a glaze layer is too thin, the color of the clay body predominates. Often a thin application can slow the development of color, texture, and opacity in the fired glaze. If a glaze layer is too thick, a glaze layer can cause the glaze to run off vertical surfaces or pool excessively in horizontal areas. Unfortunately, most glaze formulas do not contain a notation section offering information on glaze thickness or application techniques.

Decorative Engobes

An engobe, commonly called a clay slip, is a coating that masks the color and texture of a clay body. An engobe is not as glasslike as a glaze, but it can be slightly more vitreous than the clay body it covers. Engobes contain many of the same raw materials found in clay bodies and glazes, but they are used in different ratios. Engobes can be applied to ceramic pieces that are leather-hard, which shrink more than engobes applied to bisque ware. In both types of engobes, the goal is to achieve a compatible fit with the clay body.

Engobes offer the potter an alternative method of introducing color and texture to the ceramic surface.

They can be used to mask the color of the underlying clay body or introduce new color variations that can interact with covering glazes. Engobes can also respond to the kiln atmosphere in reduction, wood, salt, and soda fired kilns. In some instances, engobes can be applied thickly, resulting in a raised surface that can add another dimension to the ceramic form.

In some ways, engobes can be more difficult to apply than glazes. They have to shrink at compatible rates when applied to the clay body, and they also have to fit the covering glaze, while glazes only have to match the clay body.

A yellow engobe was applied to this platter before it was soda-fired.

ZAM WHITE ENGOBE

The ZAM White Engobe is designed to fit leather-hard clay. It can be fired from cone 06 (1,828°F [998°C]) to cone 12 (2,383° [1,306°C]). It can be used in oxidation, reduction, salt/soda, and wood kiln firing atmospheres, but its colors may vary. Be sure to test engobes on your own clay body to ensure a correct clay body and glaze fit.

Testing should involve noting any defects such as cracking or peeling of the engobe during the drying, bisque-firing, and glaze-firing stages.

ZAM White Engobe will yield a white color. For color variations, add the correct percentage of stain to the White Engobe.

ZAM White Engobe	
Clay Body	%
Grolleg kaolin	25
E.P.K.	14
Kentucky OM #4 ball clay	10
Nepheline syenite 270x	14
Flint 200x	10
Superpax	10
Soda ash	5
Ferro frit #3195	10
Vee Gum CER	2

Colored Engobe		
Color	Stain	%
Yellow	Mason stain #6404	8%
Blue	Spectrum stain #2044	10%
Pink	Spectrum stain #2083	10%
Black	Spectrum stain #2004	12%
Green	Spectrum stain #2033	10%

TIP

Note on Engobes

Always test engobes to ensure a compatible fit with the underlying clay body and the covering glaze. The clay body should be free of dust and surface particles before applying the engobe. Bisque fire the test tile. Then spray, dip, or brush on the glaze application. Place the test tile in the kiln and fire to the appropriate glaze temperature. Small test kilns may not produce accurate results, due to their faster rates of heating and cooling and lower thermal mass. Therefore, try to duplicate the same heating and cooling cycle that will be used in a larger production kiln. Additionally, fill the test kiln with pots, shelves, or posts to increase its thermal mass.

Make an Easy Engobe

Here's the simplest way to make an engobe.

Equipment

- Scale
- 80x mesh sieve
- Engobe formula

Instructions Test Batch Procedure

① Weigh the dry materials totaling 100 (3.5 oz) grams, adding approximately 90 grams (3 oz) of water. It is always better to add water in small increments to achieve the appropriate consistency. If the engobe is too thick, more water can always be added.

② Place the wet mixture through an 80x mesh sieve before applying to leather-hard clay. The engobe must be the correct consistency for the intended method of application. It should be free of coarse particles and air bubbles, be homogeneous, and remain in suspension. Engobes can be brushed, dipped or sprayed on pottery surfaces.

③ Apply to clay body.

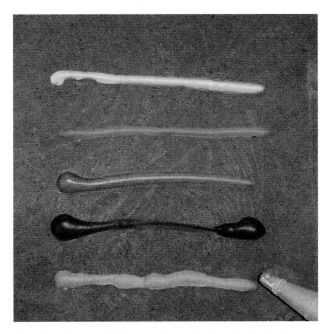

Engobes of colored clay can be applied to leather-hard, bone-dry, or bisque pottery. However, each stage of engobe application might require a different engobe formula so it will fit the underlying clay surface during the drying and firing stages.

Applying clear glaze over engobes will reveal the engobe color once the pot is fired.

TROUBLESHOOTING GLAZES

We noted symptoms of crazing and shivering during our glaze test discussions. These glaze defects and others—such as blistering—are not always easy to diagnose. Now we'll review the symptoms of blistering, crazing, and shivering and ways you can avoid these defects.

A kiln densely stacked with pottery, shelves, and posts will reduce the chance of glaze blistering (from fast heating and cooling) by increasing the thermal mass within the kiln.

Glaze blistering is also called "boiling," which is an appropriately vivid term.

Glaze Blisters

Blistering appears as a pronounced, sharp-edged burst bubble. It looks like a crater on fired glaze and often reveals the underlying clay body.

Blisters occur in some of the following kiln firing conditions.

Kiln-Firing Conditions That Cause Blistering	
Problem	Correction
Overfiring can result when any glaze is taken past its maturation temperature and lower melting point oxides within the glaze volatize. The effect is similar to water taken past its boiling point.	Firing the glaze one or two cones lower will bring it into its maturing range.
Excessively long firing in the glaze maturing range can cause volatilization of oxides, resulting in blisters. A longer time to temperature imparts additional heat work to the glaze, even if it is taken to its correct maturating temperature.	Shorten the firing cycle while still firing the glaze to its maturing range.
An excessively long cooling cycle in the glaze kiln contributes more heat work when the glaze is in the molten state, causing oxides to boil in the liquid glaze. Similar results can occur in overinsulated kilns, which allow the glaze to remain in its maturing range for extreme periods of time.	Long cooling cycles are more prevalent in hydrocarbon-fueled kilns (natural gas, propane, wood, oil, sawdust), which tend to be better insulated and larger in size, having more thermal mass than electric kilns. Upon reaching temperature, pulling the damper out and unblocking the secondary burner ports for a short time will cool the kiln faster.
Down-firing the kiln, or leaving burners or electric elements on after the glaze has reached maturity, exposes it to excessive heat work when molten.	In most instances, it is not necessary to down fire a kiln to achieve a stable glaze. However, if a particular glaze requires down firing, progressively shortening the down firing interval will decrease its time in the maturing range.

Kiln-Firing Conditions That Cause Blistering

Problem	Correction
Fast firing leaves blisters in the glaze that would have healed in a longer firing. Some glazes go through a heating period when they boil and blister on their way to maturity. If this interval is too short, blisters are "frozen" in place and do not heal. Fast firing can also trap mechanical and chemical water locked in the glaze materials, which are not completely driven off until above 932°F (500°C).	Extend the length of time to reach the end-point temperature.
Firing the glaze below its maturation range can leave a dry, pale color or blistering in the glaze surface.	Fire the glaze to its correct maturing range.
Fast firing of the bisque kiln can trap organic materials in the clay, which can then volatize during the glaze firing. The gas exits through the stiff liquid glaze, causing a blister.	A longer bisque firing cycle will enable organic material to escape.
Non-oxidation bisque firing can trap organic material in the clay, which exits at higher temperatures as a gas through the molten glaze as a blister. Large platters stacked together or tiles placed atop one another do not allow for combustion and removal of organic material because their relatively large surface areas touch.	In hydrocarbon-fueled kilns, always use more air than fuel to create an oxidation atmosphere. In electric kilns, an active venting system will remove organic matter from the kiln atmosphere.
Direct flame impingement can result in an over-fired and/or over-reduced area on a glaze, causing a blister.	Moving pottery away from the heat source will stop over-reduction and over-fired areas on the glaze.
Early and/or too heavy reduction in the glaze kiln can trap organic material in the clay or add carbon through excessive fuel introduction. Carbon trapped in the clay body can release at higher temperatures as a gas through the molten glaze, causing a blister.	Use an excess of air-to-fuel ratio in the burners until 1,860°F (1,015°C). This will remove organic matter from the clay body. Then, use a slightly reducing atmosphere until the end-point temperature is reached.
A loosely stacked glaze kiln reduces thermal mass and subsequent radiant heat in the transmission to pottery.	A densely stacked kiln can produce slower increases and decreases of temperature while radiating more heat between pottery, kiln shelves, and posts. A densely packed kiln will increase the thermal mass and apply more heat work to the glaze, which liberates gases trapped in the glaze.

Clay Body Conditions That Cause Clay Blistering

Problem	Correction
Higher than normal levels of organic material not removed from the clay during bisque firing. Periodically, some clays (notably fireclays) can contain abnormally high percentages of organic material. In such instances, a normal bisque firing cycle will not remove all the organic material from the clay. During the subsequent glaze firing, organic material carbonizes and releases as a gas through the clay body into the molten glaze, causing a blister.	A clean oxidization atmosphere in the bisque kiln, fired to the correct temperature in enough time, will release organic material from the clay.
Raw glazing an unfired clay body can drastically increase its absorbency. When glaze is applied, it can be drawn into the clay body too rapidly, causing bubbles and air pockets as the glaze dries. During firing, the bubbles migrate to the surface, causing a blister.	The use of gums such as C.M.C. (carbonxymethylcel-lulose), Vee Gum CER, or other binders (1/8 to 2 percent added to the dry weight of the glaze) can slow down the drying rate of the glaze, preventing fast absorption.
Raw glazing can trap organic matter and/or moisture in the clay body or engobe, which at higher tempera-tures exits as a gas through the glaze layer.	Slowing down the rate of heat increase in the 572°F to 1,292°F (300°C to 700°C) range can safely release visible organic materials and moisture from the clay body.
Soluble salts in the clay body can migrate to the surface as the clay dries, leaving a disruptive layer of sulfates releasing gas into the covering molten glaze.	The addition of barium carbonate (1/4 to 2 percent based on the dry weight of the clay body) can neutralize soluble salt migration.
Thin-walled pottery saturated by water during spraying, dipping, or painting during glaze application can result in blisters. Trapped moisture on the clay surface can be released as a vapor during glaze firing, causing blisters.	Use less water in the glaze batch and wait until the first glaze layer dries before applying another to prevent blisters.
Low bisque firing can yield extremely absorbent ware that sucks in the wet glaze. If the glaze is highly viscous, air pockets formed in the application process can migrate to the surface, leaving blisters in the stiff glaze.	Increase the bisque firing by one or two cones to decrease the absorbency of the pottery. Also, add gums such as C.M.C. (carbonxymethylcellulose), Vee Gum CER, or other binders to the glaze (1/8 to 2 percent based on the dry weight of the glaze) to slow down the drying rate of the glaze.
Contamination in the clay from plaster molds or deterio-rating wedging boards can impart plaster chips into the moist clay, which, upon heating, release gas and/or water vapor in the covering glaze layer.	Cover the wedging board with canvas to prevent chips from entering the clay. Mix plaster with the correct ratio of water to ensure maximum set strength. Discard plaster molds that show signs of wear to prevent plaster contami-nation in the moist clay.

Glaze Conditions that Cause Blistering

In particular, bubbles commonly form in leadless glazes, and some of these bubbles will break the surface as blisters. When lead was used in glazes, it caused a strong reactive effect with other oxides and increased the release of glaze bubbles, creating a smooth, blemish-free surface. But because lead is not a recommended glaze material, greater care must be taken in glaze formulation and application and kiln firing to ensure a defect-free glaze surface.

Problem	Correction
High-surface-tension, high-viscosity glazes that contain zirconium can trap escaping gases from other glaze materials, metallic coloring oxides, stains, gums, and binders. This type of stiff glaze is less likely to heal itself of surface irregularities, due to its inability to flow when molten.	Lower the percentage of zirconium in the glaze or substitute other opacifiers, such as titanium dioxide or tin oxide.
Cobalt oxide in an underglaze or glaze, along with copper oxide and iron oxide in reduction atmosphere, loses oxygen at 1,652°F (900°C) and can migrate through the glaze layer, causing a blister.	Slow down the rate of heat increase until 1,652°F (900°C) so oxygen in the underglaze will dissipate.
Glazes containing an overload of metallic coloring oxides in reduction kiln atmospheres can blister, due to excessive fluxing of the glaze.	Decrease the percentage of metallic coloring oxide and/or decrease the amount of reduction atmosphere in the kiln to eliminate blistering.
Contamination of the glaze with materials such as silicon carbide, wood, rust, salt, or other pottery shop materials can cause blisters.	Carefully clean and maintain the pottery shop, tools, equipment, and supplies. Always sieve the wet glaze before application to remove any unwanted particles.
An excessive amount of medium, such as C.M.C. or other gum binders, used in underglazes, engobes, glazes, or overglazes cause gas bubbles exiting as blistering in the glaze layer. The rate of fermentation, if any, is determined by the wet storage life of the materials, storage temperature, water pH, and organic materials in the mixture.	Use less medium and keep wet mixtures in cooler storage areas.
Glaze viscosity in the fluid state can promote blisters. High-viscosity stiff glazes can trap bubbles, which break at the surface, forming blisters.	Lower the viscosity by increasing the time to maturity or firing the glaze to a higher temperature. This will increase the flowing characteristics, allowing bubbles to rise to the surface, break, and heal. Also, increase the flux content of the glaze, so the mixture will flow when mature.

Problem	Correction
Excessively thick glaze applications can delay the time for bubbles to reach the glaze surface. Once bubbles are at the surface, the firing cycle can already be completed, leaving a blister.	Apply thinner layers of glaze.

Glaze Blister Q&A

As you diagnose the cause of glaze blistering, ask yourself the following questions:

Does the blistered glaze heal when fired again? A general rule for any glaze defect is that if the glaze can be refired successfully, it should have been fired longer during the first glaze firing. The second firing supplies more heat work to the glaze, which can bring it into a defect-free configuration.

Are different glaze formulas in the same kiln blistered? If yes, the problem probably originates in the firing procedures, glaze mixing errors, or a common clay or glaze raw material.

Are the blisters only on one side of the pot? If so, direct flame impingement might cause an over-fired area and/or an over-reduced area in hydrocarbon-fueled kilns. In electric kilns, the pottery could have been placed too close to the kiln elements.

Are the blisters only on overlapping glaze surfaces? Incompatible glazes when overlapped can have a eutectic effect with resulting over-fluxed areas and blisters.

Are the blisters only on horizontal surfaces? High-surface-tension glazes with high viscosity do not move when molten. Gravity on the vertical molten glaze pulls down, causing the formed blister to heal. Another possible cause occurs when flat pots are placed directly on the kiln shelf. If the glaze is not formulated or fired correctly, the radiant heat from the shelf upon cooling can cause it to remain in its maturity range longer, causing a blister.

Are the blisters only on the edges or high areas of the pots? Fast cooling of the kiln and/or pottery loosely stacked can "freeze" the glaze in its maturation process.

Are blisters present only in one kiln and not in others? This could be an indication of an error in kiln firing.

Are blisters present in only one part of the kiln? Check for direct heat source impingement or kiln atmosphere irregularities.

Are blisters present on one clay body, but not another? Check the level of organic material in the clay body. Has the clay body been bisque fired long enough in an oxidation kiln atmosphere? If the clay body contains high levels of iron-bearing clays or iron oxide, it can be more reactive to extreme reduction atmospheres produced in hydrocarbon-fueled kilns, which can cause glaze blistering.

Are blisters present only on underglaze, engobe, or overglaze areas? Check levels of gums and metallic coloring oxides in the underglaze, engobe, or overglaze. Gums during the first stages of the firing process can volatize, causing the overglaze to blister. Some metallic coloring oxides can make the underglaze, engobe, or overglaze extremely refractory, causing the glaze layer to blister.

Does the glaze have a high percentage of whiting? Whiting, calcium carbonate ($CaCO_3$), is one of the leading causes of glaze blistering. Wollastonite, which is calcium silicate ($CaSiO_3$), dissolves more readily in the molten glaze, does not release a gas, and can be substituted for whiting with an adjustment to the silica content of the glaze.

Are blisters present only on one color glaze and not on other color glazes that use the same base glaze formula? Some glazes have an excessive percentage of refractory metallic coloring oxides. Also check if the kiln atmosphere has been too heavily reduced.

Are blisters present only after a new batch of glaze is used? Often, a new bag of material is mislabeled, causing a glaze-blistering defect. Many glaze defects can be traced to incorrectly weighing out the glaze raw materials. Also, consider any kiln firing or clay body changes that might have taken place before the defect occurred.

Crazing

Understanding glaze theory is an important tool if you want to solve any glaze problem, the most common of which is crazing. Glaze crazing can happen at any temperature range and can occur in oxidation- or reduction-kiln atmospheres. Crazing occurs when glaze is under tension; it is ten times more likely to happen than shivering, which is when the glaze is under extreme compression.

Crazing presents as a series of lines or cracks in the fired glazed surface. The craze pattern can develop after removing a piece from the kiln, or it can appear years later (called delayed crazing). While crazing is classified as a glaze defect, you can correct the problem by adjusting the glaze and/or the clay body to cool at a compatible rate with the glaze coming under slight compression.

Is Correction Possible?

Before starting a correction, consider the following factors:

- The closer the craze lines, the harder the fix. If craze lines are tightly packed and close together (spaced less than $1/8$-inch [3 mm] apart), there is a decreased chance of eliminating crazing lines using this simple method. In such instances, the entire glaze formula will have to be recalculated, which is best accomplished by any one of the glaze calculation software programs that are now available (see resources section). The eight steps that follow likely will not solve the problem. Conversely, if the craze lines are wider spaced (more than $1/4$-inch [6.35 mm] apart), the fix is easier.

- Consider the absorption rate. If the clay body absorption rate exceeds 4 percent after firing, correcting crazing is more difficult.

- Try another glaze formula. If you've tried several corrections with no success and the glaze is common (such as gloss transparent, satin matte, matte, gloss blue, black, or brown) try to find a better glaze fit for the clay body.

- Choose another clay body. If you cannot change the glaze, change the clay body, with the possibility of obtaining a compatible clay body/glaze fit upon cooling.

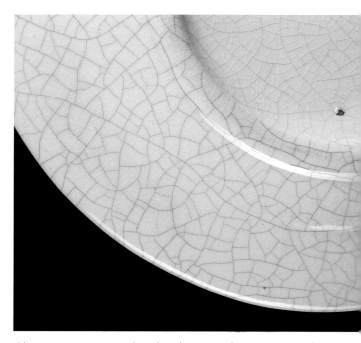

Glaze crazing occurs when the glaze is under tension (stretching on the clay body as it cools).

Crazing develops during the cooling process or after removing a piece from the kiln or, in some situations, years later, as in the case of this dish. Notice the craze stains, which resemble hairline cracks.

Glazes that are under tension when cooling in the kiln can create a fine network of stress lines called crazing, which can be visible when subjected to food or liquids.

Correcting Crazing

After considering the points on page 112, attempt a correction, or a combination of corrections, to solve glaze crazing. Depending on the severity of crazing, you may try several of these corrections until test results show craze lines moving farther apart, which is an indication that you are alleviating the problem. The following eight steps are not the only crazing corrections available, but they have shown consistent results.

Equipment

- Gram scale
- Glaze bucket
- Mixing spoon

Instructions

① Most flint used in glazes comes in 200, 325, and 400 mesh. Finer-grind sizes might be available on special order from a ceramics supplier. Also try fused silica, which has been calcined (fired) and has a very low shrinkage rate, which will help stop crazing. Most glaze formulas can accommodate additions of flint, without the glaze becoming opaque or dry when fired. Try additions of 10, 20, and 25 units of measure. For instance, if the glaze has 50 grams of flint, increase flint to 60 grams, 70 grams, and 75 grams. Do not change the other glaze materials.

② Prolong the last third of the glaze firing by two to three hours. This will give the clay body the best chance to tighten up, or reach its maturity, which will help in achieving a good glaze fit. The kiln should be fully loaded with pottery or shelves and posts to ensure greater thermal mass and increased radiant heat transmission.

③ By firing higher and/or longer, the glaze and clay body have a better chance of maturing for a better fit. Remember, what must change is the rate of shrinkage in the clay body, glaze, or both, which results in the glaze being under slight compression. However, if the clay body is already over-fired or on the edge of its maturity range, firing higher will cause more crazing in the glaze.

④ Add flint 200x mesh to the clay body. Increase flint by 5, 10, and 15 units of measure. Flint found in clay bodies remains a crystalline solid that has different characteristics than flint in a glaze, but it will still work to stop crazing in a glaze.

⑤ The kiln should be cool enough to unload pottery without gloves. Waiting for the kiln to cool will cause no problems; fast cooling increases the chance of crazing. If the pots are "pinging" when you open the kiln door, the glaze is under stress and is more likely to craze.

⑥ When using a low-fire clay body, bisque-firing one or two cones higher will bring the glaze under slight compression, preventing crazing.

⑦ The ceramics supplier or the manufacturer of the frit will have the coefficient of expansion rates for each frit. Materials with low coefficients of expansion (for example, flint) are less likely to cause crazing.

⑧ A thinner coat is not an option for all glazes, but even a slight decrease in thickness can stop crazing. Still, a thinner application does not address the underlying cause of crazing, which is the glaze being under tension as it cools on the clay body.

① Add increasing amounts of flint to the glaze formula.

② Fire the kiln to the correct temperature over a longer time.

③ Fire the kiln one or two pyrometric cones higher, but only if the glaze or clay body will not be adversely affected.

④ If many different types of glazes are crazing on the same clay body, first adjust the clay body.

⑤ Slowly cool the glaze kiln. Do not open the kiln door until the temperature is below 200°F (93°C).

⑥ If you use a low-fire body and the glaze begins to craze, try bisque firing one or two cones higher than the recommended glaze firing temperature.

⑦ If the glaze contains frit and is crazing, try using a frit with a lower coefficient of expansion.

⑧ Crazing can often be eliminated by applying a thinner glaze.

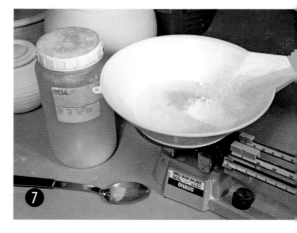

Shivering

Shivering is the opposite problem from crazing. Though statistically not as common as other defects, when shivering occurs, it can spoil the functionality of glaze on pottery. Shivering forms when a glaze is under too great a compressive load as it cools in the kiln, resulting in the glaze being too large for the underlying clay body. The defect looks like a paint chip peeling off the underlying clay body. Sometimes, shivering can reveal itself years later because the clay body/glaze combination is under constant stress. When the glaze is under extreme compression, it can buckle any time. While shivering is classified as a glaze defect, it can be corrected either through adjusting the glaze, clay body formula, or a combination of both.

Shivering can happen at any temperature range, and it can occur in oxidation- or reduction-kiln atmospheres. Frequently, glaze starts peeling on the edges or raised areas of the clay. Chips of shivered glaze range from $^1/16$ inch (2 mm) to 2 inches (5 cm). Tapping seemingly stable clay/glaze surfaces with a hard object will cause a glazed area to flake off, sometimes removing part of the supporting clay body. The goal of any correction is to cool the clay body and glaze at a compatible rate, with the glaze coming under slight compression.

Shivering Fixes

Consider the following points before attempting to fix a glaze shivering defect.

- Clay body formulas containing too much free silica can cause shivering. Fireclays are known to have randomly high levels of free silica. Fine-grind grog that is high in silica also can cause shivering, especially if it's burnished or rubbed into the clay surface during the forming process. Low-expansion-rate, lithium-based feldspars used in clay bodies such as petalite, lithospar, lepidolite, or spodumene can cause shivering in glazes with higher-expansion-rate potassium and sodium-based feldspars used in glazes.

- Reduction causes instability and, therefore, shivering. Too much and/or too early reduction in a clay body causes an unstable carbon bond between the clay and glaze layer that can result in shivering.

- Thick glaze aggravates shivering. If any or all of the aforementioned conditions are present, a thick glaze application can exacerbate shivering. Apply a thinner layer of glaze to resolve symptoms, understanding that this "fix" will not alter the underlying cause of extreme glaze compression.

Above, shivering occurred at the base of this bowl, resulting in a peeled-paint look that indicates glaze under stress. At left, shivering glaze flakes off of the fired bowl, revealing the underlying clay body.

Other Methods

Keep in mind, some corrections can change glaze color, texture, light transmission, or maturing range. Other less practical methods for correcting shivering include the following:

- Lowering the maximum firing temperature
- A firing faster to the glaze maturation point.
- Reducing the amount of lime or iron in the clay body to improve the glaze/clay body fit
- Substituting a sodium feldspar for a potash feldspar, because sodium feldspars have a higher coefficient of expansion (high shrinkage).

Correct Shivering

In most instances, shivering can be corrected by adding sodium- or potassium-based feldspar, frit, or other high-expansion materials to the glaze, provided the clay body does not contain lithium-based feldspars. When shivering is very severe (glaze under extreme compression), it can tear or break the underlying clay body, causing the whole piece to crack apart upon cooling.

Other shivering correction methods involve adding high-expansion materials to the clay body and/or glaze (feldspars or other alkali bearing materials) or decreasing low-expansion materials in clay bodies and glazes, such as flint, petalite, lepidolite, lithospar, spodumene, and glazes with high amounts of lithium carbonate. Sometimes a combination of all these methods is necessary.

Equipment

- Gram scale
- Glaze bucket
- Mixing spoon

Instructions

① If only one glaze is shivering on the clay body, correct shivering by adding 5, 10, or 15 units of measure of sodium- or potassium-based feldspar to the glaze. Or, add other alkali-bearing materials. (For example, if the glaze has 10 grams of feldspar, increase feldspar to 15, 20, and 25 grams. Do not change the amounts of other materials in the glaze formula.) Adding any flux or glass former will increase the chance of the glaze becoming glossy or running off vertical surfaces. The ideal fix is to get just enough feldspar or frit into the glaze to correct shivering but not overload the glaze with more flux than needed.

② Decrease the flint in a glaze by 5 or 10 units to adjust the clay body/glaze fit.

③ Add sodium- or potassium-based feldspar/frit to a glaze and take out flint from the glaze. In rare instances, this correction must also be carried out in the clay body.

④ If many different types of glazes are shivering on the same clay body, start the correction by adding 5, 10, and 15 units of sodium- or potassium-based feldspar (or other alkali-bearing materials) to the clay body.

⑤ Decrease flint in the clay body by 5 or 10 units.

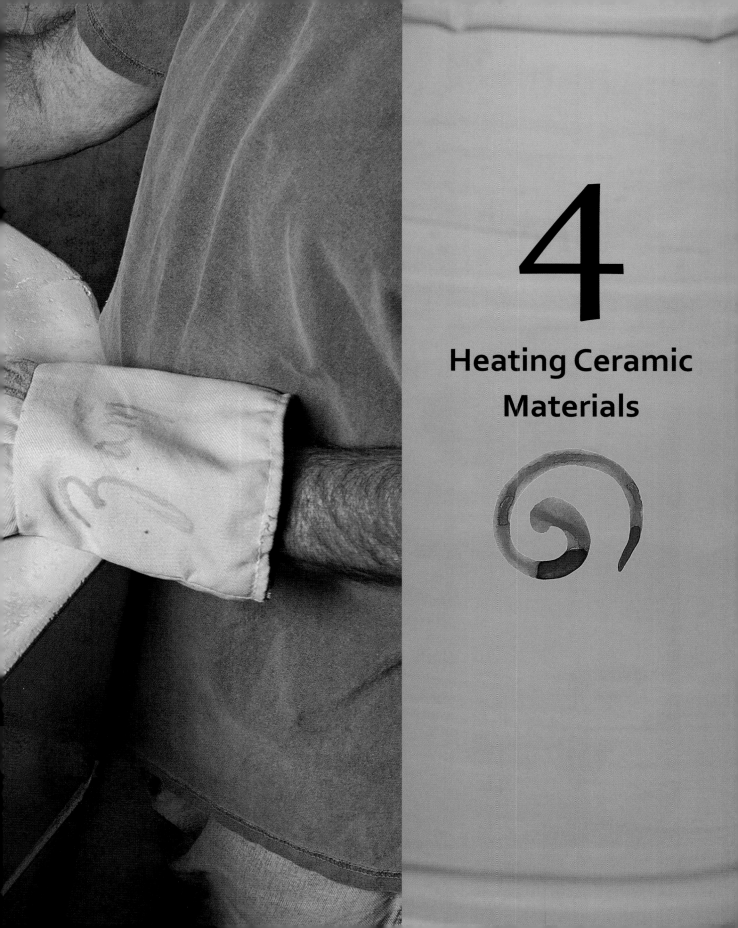

4

Heating Ceramic Materials

INSIDE THE KILN

Most miscalculations in the ceramic process occur during firing. Many clay body and glaze defects can be directly related to faults in the kiln's heating and cooling cycle. For a thorough and diverse knowledge of kiln firing, fire as many different kilns as possible, rather than learning to just fire one. Craft centers and college ceramics departments offer the best locations for this experience.

Wheel-Thrown Bottle
9" (22.9 cm) tall, 4" (10.2 cm) diameter
Firing: cone 9 (2,300°F [1,260°C]),
reduction atmosphere
See page 158 for formula

Conduction

Conduction is the transfer of energy through matter (as in the movement of heat from an atom).

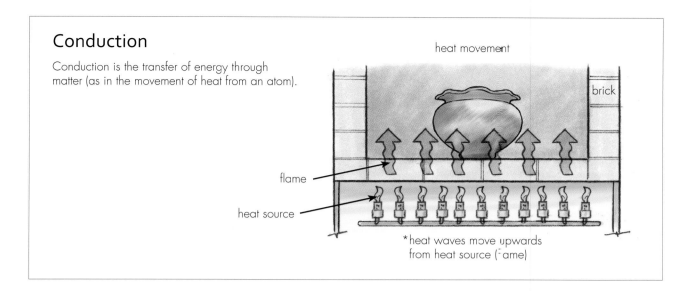

heat movement

brick

flame

heat source

*heat waves move upwards from heat source (flame)

Convection

The process by which heat is transferred through the movement of air. This method of heat transfer can be felt when opening a hot oven. Air molecules are heated from the heat source and then move about the kiln, heating the interior of the kiln, shelves, and pots.

Convection is the transfer of heat through mass-movement of either air or water.

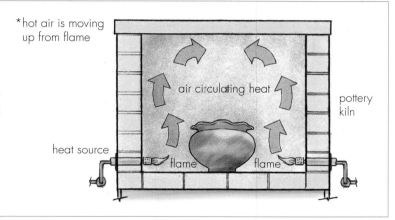

*hot air is moving up from flame

air circulating heat

heat source

pottery kiln

flame   flame

Radiation

Heat is transferred through the kiln by energy waves. When a kiln is heated, it generates thermal mass in the kiln from kiln bricks, shelves, posts, and pots. The radiant heat is transferred to every object in the kiln. After the heat source is turned off, radiant heat still affects all objects in the kiln.

Radiation comprises electromagnetic waves that move energy directly through space (as the Sun's rays transport heat to the Earth).

*heat waves are radiating inward from the outside of the kiln

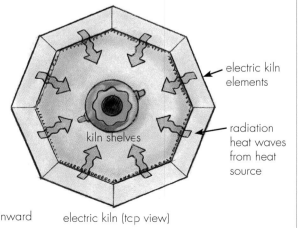

electric kiln elements

radiation heat waves from heat source

kiln shelves

electric kiln (top view)

Heating a Kiln

Heat is a form of energy produced by the movement of molecules, capable of transmission through convection, conduction, or radiation.

Conduction: The transfer of heat through solids. When the kiln is fired, kiln shelves gather and release heat during and after the firing. The heat is transferred directly through the solid kiln shelf, posts, and other pots on the shelf. When the heat source is turned off, the overall kiln temperature drops, but the kiln shelves and other kiln furniture act as a thermal reserve, transferring heat to pottery on the shelf. Some materials transfer conduction heat more efficiently than other materials. (Anyone who has touched a pizza stone fresh from the oven has experienced burning conduction heating first-hand.) There is still a great amount of heat stored within the hard brick shelf, which takes a while to dissipate.

Melting Characteristics

Ceramic materials react or melt under specific conditions. The absolute, or end-point temperature is the most common factor causing clay and glazes to melt. The higher the temperature for any given ceramic material, the greater the degree of melting that takes place in the clay body or glaze. Glass formation (called vitrification) occurs when fluxing materials react with alumina and silica in clay and glazes. However, other factors that contribute to melting may not be so apparent to potters firing their kilns.

Convection: The process by which heat is transferred through the movement of air. This method of heat transfer can be felt when opening a hot oven. Air molecules are heated from the heat source and then move about the kiln, heating the interior of the kiln, shelves, and pots.

Radiation: Heat is transferred through the kiln by energy waves. When a kiln is heated, it generates thermal mass in the kiln from kiln bricks, shelves, posts, and pots. The radiant heat is transferred to every object in the kiln. After the heat source is turned off, radiant heat still affects all objects in the kiln.

Particle size: The particle size of ceramic materials also can affect the melting characteristics of glazes and clay body formulas. The smaller the particle size, the greater the melting potential of any ceramic material. Small particle sizes expose greater surface areas to heat.

Kiln atmosphere: Depending on the heating source, a kiln can be fired in oxidation, neutral, or reduction atmospheres. An electric kiln produces an oxidation-kiln atmosphere because the ratio of air is higher than fuel. In reduction-kiln atmospheres, the ratio of fuel-to-air is higher, producing carbon monoxide. This colorless and odorless gas is oxygen-hungry. When the gas is in the presence of easily reduced metallic coloring oxides found in clays and glazes, it draws an oxygen molecule from them, changing their color and lowering their melting characteristics. Other oxides found in clay and glaze formulas are not so easily reduced and need higher temperatures than pottery kilns can economically achieve.

Eutectics: These are combinations of two or more materials that cause melting at the lowest possible temperature. Eutectics can be formed when different oxides are brought together in glazes. The most common example is lead and silica. When the mixture is heated, it produces a lower melting point than lead or silica melted separately. A strong eutectic can develop when two or more glazes are overlapped on a pot. The mixture of glazes can cause blistering, pinholes, or glaze running off vertical surfaces, as well as pooling excessively in horizontal areas.

Metallic coloring oxides: Iron oxide, for example, can act as a strong flux (melting agent) in glaze if used in high percentages. On the opposite end of the spectrum is chrome oxide, which is a refractory or heat-resistant oxide. High percentages of chrome oxide can dry the surface texture of the fired glaze. Other metallic coloring oxides, to various degrees, can be classified as contributing a refractory or flux component to clay body or glazes.

Clay body: A clay body that is absorbent when fired can leach out fluxing oxides in the melting glaze during the firing. A dry surface texture and/or glaze opacity can result when some portion of the flux oxides in the glaze are leached into the clay body surface.

Glaze thickness: Whether a glaze is sprayed, dipped, or brushed on the ceramic surface, the actual thickness of the glaze can play an important part in its ability to melt. As a general rule, the thinner the glaze layer, the greater degree of melting. A thick glaze application can need more heat work (the time it takes to arrive at the maturing temperature of the glaze) to cause complete vitrification (glass formation) of the entire glaze layer.

Glaze application technique is critical for functional pottery, whether sprayed, dipped (like this piece), or brushed, in order to achieve a smooth defect-free fired surface.

When overlapping one glaze with another there is always the possibility that the glaze materials will be incompatible due to an eutectic reaction, which can cause glaze blistering or dripping in the overlapped area.

Pyrometric Cone and Temperature Equivalents

Use this chart to determine the firing temperature for clays and glazes. The chart provides temperature equivalents for self-supporting large pyrometric cones fired at a rate of 180°F (100°C) per hour at the end of the firing. Courtesy of the Edward Orton Jr. Ceramic Foundation.

CONE	FAHRENHEIT (°)	CELSIUS (°)
022	1087	586
021	1112	600
020	1159	626
019	1252	678
018	1319	715
017	1360	738
016	1422	772
015	1456	791
014	1485	807
013	1539	837
012	1582	861
011	1607	875
010	1657	903
09	1688	920
08	1728	942
07	1789	976
06	1828	998
05 ½	1859	1015
05	1888	1031
04	1945	1063
03	1987	1086
02	2016	1102
01	2046	1119
1	2079	1137
2	2088	1142
3	2106	1152
4	2124	1162
5	2167	1186
5 ½	2197	1203
6	2232	1222
7	2262	1239
8	2280	1249
9	2300	1260
10	2345	1285
11	2361	1294
12	2383	1306
13	2428	1331
14	2489	1365

The Kiln at Work

The heating and cooling cycle in a kiln firing can affect how clay and glaze materials melt. We refer to heating cycles and the stages of firing as "heat work." A significant amount of heat work must occur before the kiln reaches its end-point temperature. The kiln heats in stages, the first being a bisque firing. This prepares the clay for future glazing. The pot is fired again after glazing.

The three most common temperature ranges used to produce pottery and sculptures are: low fire, cone 06 (1,828°F [998°C]); medium fire, cone 6 (2,232°F [1,222°C]); and high fire, cone 9 (2,300°F [1,260°C]). Each temperature range has several qualities that can be beneficial to the function or aesthetic considerations of the ceramic object. Low-fire temperature ranges can produce

glaze finishes in bright, crisp colors. Firing kilns to low temperature also enables faster heating and cooling cycles and less wear on kiln shelves, posts, and bricks.

The medium- to high-temperature ranges produce dense, glass-like, hard ceramic clay bodies and glazes. Clay and glaze may be integrated more fully when heated to medium or high temperatures. The greater interface development produces glazes that look integral to the clay body surface, as opposed to a "painted–on" superficial glaze coating found in low temperature clay body and glaze ranges. However, there are several exceptions where low fire-clay bodies can be formulated to create dense, nonabsorbent ceramic forms.

Slower bisque-firing times are necessary if pots are thicker than ½ inch (1.3 cm) or taller than 14 inches (36 cm). Longer bisque firing times are essential if plates, tiles,

Kiln Heat Work

As the kiln temperature rises, clay body and glaze undergo chemical changes that dictate the quality of the final product.

Temperature	Chemical Change
212° to 392°F (100° to 200°C)	Mechanical or free water is removed from the clay body.
842° to 1,112°F (450°C to 600°C)	Chemically combined water is removed; shrinkage can occur during this temperature range.
1,063°F (573°C)	Quartz or flint components of clay body expand.
572° to 1,292°F (300° to 700°C)	Organic matter in clay is oxidized and removed; if the kiln is not fired in a complete oxidation atmosphere, carbon can cause bloating in the clay body at higher temperatures.
1,796°F (980°C)	Metakcolin, an intermediate product formed when kaolin is heated, changes to spinel, which ejects silica.
1,922° to 2,012°F (1,050° to 1,100°C)	Spinel changes to mullite; feldspar melts; vitrified clay body reacts with silica ejected in spinel/mullite formation.
2,195°F (1,202°C)	Clay body porosity decreases sharply.
2,012° to 2,282°F (1,100° to 1,250°C)	Silica or quartz in the clay body starts to change to cristobalite. If high amounts of cristobalite are formed in the clay body at this point, it can cause cooling cracks in the 392°F (200°C) temperature range. Cristobalite cracking in clay bodies is often encountered when a kiln stalls or takes an exceptionally long time after cone 8 (2,280°F [1,249°C]) to reach its final firing temperature.

wide-based forms, or thicker forms are fired. A common firing mistake is firing functional pottery at a "safe" bisque-firing cycle, then firing plates or large sculptural pieces with the same cycle. The plates or larger pieces often crack or blow up, throwing small shards throughout the kiln. Larger and/or thicker pieces need slower temperature increases to safely release their mechanical and chemical water. Play with temperature settings and choose appropriate heating cycles for the work you are firing.

Firing Too Fast

A clay body can be strong and durable with the right clay body formula, appropriate end-point temperature, and correct time to temperature. A fast-fired clay body has not achieved its maximum strength potential. The clay might look dense, but functional pottery that is fast-fired often breaks or cracks in normal, daily use.

On the other hand, an overfired clay body can slump, bloat, shrink excessively, stick to the kiln shelf, or warp. If a kiln is fired to increasingly higher temperatures, any clay body can be eventually transformed into a glaze.

A fast kiln firing can affect glazes in several visible ways, resulting in a dry, rough, or dull surface texture, immediate glaze crazing, pinholes, blisters, a muted or dull glaze color, and a less durable glaze surface. Fast firing also can increase solubility in a glaze, which results in staining on plates or functional pots. A "soft" glaze surface might look perfect, but it can be easily scratched and dulled by abrasive cleaners or alkaline dishwasher liquids.

Any clay body can slump or deform past its maturing range, due to firing. Depending on the amount of overfiring, the pottery can warp, stick to the kiln shelves, or deform into a horizontal mass.

Take Your Time

A kiln can be programmed to hold at a specific temperature for a period of time. Holding at temperature increases melting, because the materials are given more heat work, resulting in greater glass formation. If you choose to hold at the maturing temperature of the glaze, there is always the possibility of boiling off lower constituent glaze oxides. This causes glaze blisters, running, or clay body bloating. The safe approach is not to hold the glaze at temperature. Instead, fire to the glaze-maturing temperature over a longer period of time. Or, down-fire the kiln, which delays the cooling cycle of the kiln. In electric kilns, down-firing can be achieved simply by turning on the element switches to low or medium after the kiln has reached its end-point temperature. In hydrocarbon-fueled kilns, such as natural gas or propane, leave the burners on a low setting after the kiln has reached its end-point temperature. Both techniques will expand the heating and cooling curve of the kiln firing.

Kiln Types and Considerations

The type of fuel used to fire the kiln can be a determining factor in studio location and the overall cost of producing pottery.

Kilns fired by hydrocarbon-based fuels such as natural gas, propane, wood, coal, or oil might require permits from the local fire department as well as a survey of neighbors for potential objections. For example, kilns require enough space for the potter to easily walk around for inspections during the firing process. Hydrocarbon-fueled kilns also require a room large enough to facilitate fresh air circulation to assist and then remove the products of combustion within the kiln. Also plan for the kiln stack and its exit through the roof structure.

The proximity of neighbors and the gases exiting from the stack during a firing are significant factors in kiln and subsequent stack location. Some potential studio kiln locations might be off-limits, due to local zoning restrictions or individuals and businesses that do not want a pottery close by. Research the existing area and the neighborhood. Kilns fired by propane require a storage tank. Consider placement of the tank, which can be large, in relation to the kiln and your outside surroundings.

Electric kilns should be installed by professional electricians. You need dedicated circuit breakers for each kiln used in the studio and sufficient electrical capacity to power kilns, equipment, and tools.

Active venting of the kilns to an outside source is also recommended to ensure a safe studio atmosphere. The fumes from improperly vented electric kilns can drift into the studio and other building occupants, causing complaints and possible legal action for eviction. Even outdoor electric kilns can require venting, depending on their location, to safely remove exhaust from the immediate environment or prevent exhaust from endangering other areas.

Kiln Size

Many potters use electric kilns for bisque firing their ware and gas kilns for glaze firing. On average, you can fill a kiln with 40 cubic feet (1.1 m3) of usable stacking space with 65 to 120 functional pots, depending on their size. Use these figures as a starting point for planning the kiln size that will fit your production requirements.

If you're interested in selling your wares, consider estimating the wholesale versus retail price of pots contained in a single kiln firing. Smaller kilns offer greater flexibility to meet production schedules or custom orders, but they are labor-intensive for stacking, firing, and unloading. On the other hand, larger kilns offer the economy of scale, because it takes just as much effort to fire a large kiln as it does to fire a small kiln. Ask for advice from other potters before you purchase or build a kiln.

A wood-kiln-fired pot (such as the pot in the middle below) allows ash deposits to fall on exposed pottery surfaces. Gas-kiln-fired pottery (such as the cup at right) offers reduction, oxidation, or neutral atmosphere options or combinations of atmospheres during the firing, all of which can change the color of the clay body and glaze. Electric-kiln-firing can produce consistent clay body and glaze colors (such as in the mug at left).

Wheel-Thrown Disk
2 1/2" (5.7 cm) tall, 9"
(22.9 cm) wide
Firing: cone 04
(1,945°F [1,063°C]),
oxidation atmosphere
(electric kiln)
See page 158 for formula

Kiln Safety

All kilns require careful attention to safety. Different types of kilns, however, have specific safety requirements.

Wood-fired kilns require constant stoking to achieve a steady temperature increase. They also require a dry storage area for stacking wood that will be used in the firing. Large kilns might need one or more cords of wood per firing, depending on their size. It is not unusual for the firings to last two or three days.

Always observe the following safety considerations: Store the wood away from any possible heat sources. Keep the immediate areas around the wood-fired kiln free of any hazards that can cause injury to potters firing the kiln. Wear heat-resistant gloves for stoking the kiln and to prevent wood splinters. Someone should be present to monitor the entire firing process. A rotating staff is best, because the wood-firing process can be time-consuming, labor-intensive, and tiring.

Gas-fired kilns need monitoring and should be checked at frequent intervals to ensure appropriate temperature increases and the correct atmospheric environment for the ware.

Electric kilns can be programmed to fire automatically, but the safety aspects of being present during any kiln firing operation cannot be overlooked. An automatic shut-off device can turn off a kiln at the end of a firing, but you should not rely completely on this mechanism. If the shut-off device fails, all pots would be lost and the kiln damaged.

FIRING METHODS

The type of kiln used in firing pottery, whether it produces an oxidation, neutral, or reduction atmosphere, can influence the fired color of the clay body and glaze. This 10 inch-high covered jar was fired in a natural-gas, sprung arch, 20-cu/ft. car kiln, cone 9 (2,300°F [1,260 °C]) reduction atmosphere.

Kiln Atmosphere

Kiln atmosphere and special effects, such as brushing clay slip onto pottery or staining with metallic coloring oxides, allow the potter to express personality in each piece. The kiln-firing atmosphere changes all clay body colors.

Hydrocarbon-fueled kilns are also less expensive to build and fire as their cubic-foot dimensions increase, as compared with electric kilns of similarly large dimensions. For example, the cost to build and fire an 80-cubic-foot (2.3-m³) electric kiln will cost more than building and firing a natural gas- or propane-fired kiln of the same dimensions. Either of these kilns can be hand-built or purchased from kiln manufacturers for approximately one-third more in cost.

Smaller electric kilns (5 cubic feet to 12 cubic feet [141 L to 339 L]) are easily purchased through many ceramics suppliers. They can be installed in many locations, such as pottery studios or home basements. Note that electric kilns usually require additional electrical output. Electric kilns offer flexibility in a production firing schedule because you can purchase more than one kiln. Electric kilns are accurate and efficient, and many are now computer-controlled, allowing for easy operation. Keep in mind, that an electric kiln's atmosphere is limited to oxidation, which means using a limited range of clay body formulas and glaze colors and textures.

Reduction Atmosphere

A reduction atmosphere is created when excess hydrocarbon fuels (natural gas, propane, wood, oil, or methane) to air ratios are present in a kiln, creating carbon monoxide, an oxygen-hungry, colorless, and odorless gas. While there is still enough oxygen present for combustion to take place, the amount of carbon monoxide present pulls or draws an oxygen component away from specific oxides found in the clay body and glazes. In reduction-kiln firing conditions, the primary metallic coloring oxides of iron, rutile (iron and titanium naturally combined), and manganese flux to a greater degree than would occur in an oxidation-kiln atmosphere. Here are some points about reduction-kiln firing to keep in mind.

- Reduction affects metallic coloring oxides, such as copper, zinc, nickel cobalt, iron, and manganese.

- Reduction does not affect alumina, vanadium, titanium, cerium, barium, magnesium, chromium, calcium, sodium, potassium, and silica at the temperatures reached in craft-pottery kilns.

- Hydrocarbon-based fuels (containing water, sulfur dioxide, and sulfur trioxide) can create carbon monoxide and carbon dioxide when heated. Byproducts, trace fuel elements, oxygen, moisture, and nitrogen in the kiln subtly affect clay body color. The clay body color transformation is most noticeable in reduction-fired clay bodies containing iron-bearing clays or clays containing metallic coloring oxides, such as manganese, rutile, nickel, copper oxide, and chrome oxide. For example, ferric iron oxide present in a clay body, when subjected to a reduction-kiln atmosphere (carbon monoxide atmosphere caused by more fuel than air present in the combustion process), produces a gray clay body color when covered by a glaze as the iron is transformed into a ferrous state.

- Clay body color also can be achieved by trapping carbon in the clay during the early stages of reduction-kiln firing. The effect is achieved by introducing more fuel (wood, natural gas, propane, oil) into the kiln than air. Carbon is then trapped in the clay body, causing a gray to black color. This technique has been practiced in raku firing, pit firing, and high-temperature-range Shino glazes, in which carbon is trapped below the vitrified glaze surface.

Carbon-trap Shino glaze fired at cone 9 (2,300°F [1,250°C])

This iron-bearing stoneware clay was fired in a reduction atmosphere to cone 9 (2,300°F [1,260°C]). Upon cooling, the reduced iron reoxidizes to a brown color.

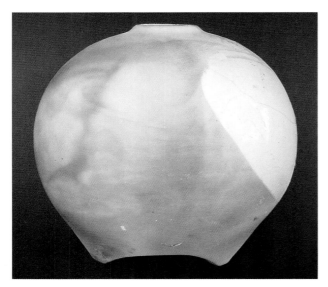

This pit-fired pot has a carbon flashing pattern on the unglazed clay body.

Pit Firing

Pit firing is a so-called primitive method of imparting color to a clay body surface. Pots are placed in an earthen pit with combustible materials. The pots can either be fired bone-dry, or they can be bisque fired first to prevent cracking in the subsequent, sometimes uneven, heating encountered in pit firing. During the pit-firing process, carbon from excessive fuel-to-air ratios is randomly drawn through the firing chamber where the pots are placed. Carbon is then impregnated into the porous unglazed areas of the clay body, causing random patterns of black to gray flashing. Areas not affected by carbon remain in their original light color.

Neutral Atmosphere

Neutral kiln atmospheres are the middle stage on a continuum of firing atmospheres that use hydrocarbon fuels, ranging from oxidation to reduction. A neutral kiln atmosphere occurs in a hydrocarbon-based fueled kiln when there is an equal air-to-gas ratio to achieve combustion. Neutral kiln atmospheres can yield different colors in clay bodies and glazes, depending on the base materials in the clay or glaze formula and the addition of metallic coloring oxides or stains. Neutral kiln atmospheres produced by hydrocarbon-based fuels, such as oil, propane, or natural gas, can introduce trace amounts of water, sulfur, or other elements found in the fuel. These trace elements can affect clay body or glaze color response.

Oxidation Atmosphere

Oxidation atmospheres can take place in hydrocarbon-based fueled kilns or electric kilns. All that must be present is an air-to-fuel ratio where air exceeds fuel. In electric-fired kilns, an oxidation atmosphere is a given and is always present, provided there is no source of combustible material in the kiln. Clay bodies may fire to different colors in oxidation hydrocarbon-based fuel kilns than in electric kilns. These color changes are caused by moisture and trace elements found in hydrocarbon-based fuels. For example,

Diagram of a Pit-Fired Kiln

combustible material

pottery

earth

A pit kiln filled with combustible materials with pots inside.

iron oxide in a clay body can produce muted cream colors in an oxidation atmosphere. The same clay fired in a reduction kiln atmosphere could produce various shades of brown/reds.

In oxidation atmospheres, clay bodies containing manganese dioxide, either in the powder or granular form, are muted in color. Often, granular manganese is visible as light brown specks in the fired clay body. Low iron-bearing clays in oxidation-kiln atmospheres can show vibrant colors with the addition of metallic coloring oxides or stains. The same clay body formula in a reduction-kiln atmosphere shows muted colors because of iron or manganese present in the clay body.

Salt-and-soda fired pottery has a traditional "orange peel" pebble surface texture on exposed clay body surfaces. Clay body and glaze color variations can occur in a wood-fired kiln, due to kiln atmosphere conditions during the firing.

TIP

Surface Deposits

Wood-fired pottery can expose the clay body surface to ash deposits and variations in kiln atmosphere occurring during the firing. Salt- or soda-firing releases sodium vapors into the kiln during the firing process, which forms a sodium/alumina/silicate glaze on the clay body.

Wood, Soda, and Salt Kiln Atmospheres

Wood, soda, or salt kilns can change the clay body color. They introduce kiln conditions that promote clay color variations. Wood, salt, or soda can be added in reduction, neutral, or oxidation atmospheres. Each firing atmosphere produces a distinct color effect on clay.

Wood: Because of uneven stoking and combustion of wood in the kiln, the atmosphere can shift among oxidation, neutral, and reduction. The result is clay color variations and flashing areas on the exposed clay surfaces. Wood ash combines at high temperature with the alumina and silica present on unglazed areas of the clay body to produce an alkaline glaze, which can tint the clay body color light tan, brown, or gray, depending on the ash deposit depth on the ware and kiln atmosphere.

Salt and soda: In reduction-kiln atmospheres, firing with salt or soda causes a reaction with the alumina and silica in the clay body. The result is a sodium/alumina/silicate glaze. The glaze seals in the black ferrous oxide in the clay body, producing a gray clay body color. The same gray color is also prevalent in wood-fired kilns because alkaline ash lands on the clay body. That ash forms a sealing glaze, preventing iron that is present in the clay body from reoxidizing to a brown ferric oxide color as oxygen enters the cooling kiln.

TIP

Bisque firing is an intermediate stage in the firing process, allowing the easy application of glaze. Often the bisque-fired color does not represent the final fired color of the clay body.

Soda/salt firing to cone 9 (2,300°F [1,260°C]) produces an "orange peel" pebbly-effect glaze. See page 159 for formula

Changing Clay Color

The individual properties of a clay body formula, kiln atmosphere, firing temperature, and special effects all work together to produce the fired clay body color. Each factor can have a major or minor influence on the final outcome of a fired piece of ceramic material. While clay body color variations are infinite, you can change the color of a clay body through firing techniques.

The clay body formula itself is a critical element in determining the fired color of the clay. Iron oxide is one of the strongest metallic coloring-producing agents found in clays. It is also very sensitive to changes in kiln atmosphere, which can bring about a color change in the clay body. You can incorporate iron oxide into a clay body formula by adding raw ore (the synthetic oxide form of iron oxide) or iron-bearing clays. Iron oxide is a strong flux, and when used in high percentages in the clay body, it can cause over-vitrification, resulting in bloating, slumping, and excessive clay warping in the fired state.

Other oxide components in the clay body formula can contribute to a lighter or darker fired color in the clay body. Clays containing iron and titanium dioxide with low percentages of alumina (less than 23 percent) will exhibit darker fired colors than clays containing iron and titanium, in which higher amounts of alumina in the clay cause increased mullite in the firing, which masks the fired color. Ball clays are composed of approximately 75 percent kaolinite ($Al_2O_3 \cdot 2\ SiO_2 \cdot 2\ H_2O$), which will fire darker than kaolins, which contain approximately 95 percent kaolinite and correspondingly fewer impurities, such as iron and titanium.

Manganese dioxide can also have a profound effect on the color of clay bodies. Manganese dioxide in various concentrations and particle sizes is often found in fireclays, ball clays, and stoneware clays. Manganese dioxide granules can cause black/brown specking in fired clay.

Speking Effect

If you fire an electric kiln, you can duplicate the specking that occurs in reduction atmospheres by adding granular manganese dioxide 60x mesh to the clay body.

Equipment

- Moist clay
- $\frac{1}{2}$ percent manganese dioxide
- 60x mesh

Instructions

① Add $\frac{1}{2}$ percent of manganese dioxide screened through a 60x mesh sieve (based on a total clay body of 100 percent) to the moist clay. This will result in approximately 200 specks per square inch in the fired clay surface. Form pottery by hand building or wheel work.

② Fire the finished pottery in an electric kiln. To see the specks, fire the clay body to maturity, which means the clay will be dense, hard, and vitreous when removed from the kiln.

Note: This speckling effect often looks uniform in the size and spacing of the specking, unlike the typical random specking found in clay bodies fired in a reduction-kiln atmosphere. Be careful. In some instances, the manganese can cause bloating in the fired clay body because part of the manganese goes off as a gas during the firing.

Granular, 60x mesh manganese dioxide sieved into the moist clay can produce black specking in the fired clay body.

White clay bodies often reveal the additions of metallic coloring oxides or stains better than dark bodies.

Dark-firing clay body formulas, which already contain high percentages of iron-bearing clays, can produce even darker fired color clays when metallic coloring oxides or stains are added to the clay body. For example, adding cobalt oxide to a clay body containing high percentages of iron-bearing clay will result in a black clay body color. Additions of metallic coloring oxides or stains to a clay body are also subject to the effects of the kiln atmosphere and temperature, which can produce many variations in color intensity.

Special Glaze Effects

As you experiment with clay body formulas, try these special effects that involve adding stain washes, metallic oxides, and clay slips.

Metallic oxide/stain wash: Try combining coloring oxides and their carbonate forms with water and paint the mixture on a raw or bisque-fired clay body to impart color to the fired clay.

> **Coloring oxides:** rutile, copper oxide, cobalt oxide, manganese dioxide, iron oxide, or chrome oxide
> **Carbonate forms:** copper carbonate, cobalt carbonate, or manganese carbonate.

Clay Handling Characteristics

Adding oxides can affect the clay's handling characteristics. Here's how:

Metallic coloring oxides can affect the handling characteristics of moist clay. Adding red iron oxide to a clay body can produce a darker fired color. However, high percentages of iron oxide (more than 2 to 5 percent, based on the dry weight of the clay body) can cause moist clay to slump in forming operations and become gummy when moist.

Iron oxide can act as a flux (melting agent), forming with other clay body fluxes, such as feldspar. The result is increased vitrification, shrinkage, bloating, and deformation in the fired piece. In reduction-firing conditions, increased percentages of iron oxide can cause brittle fired clay with low tensile strength. Iron oxide can be mixed with water, creating a wash. A watercolor-consistency iron oxide wash can be applied to the leather-hard, bone-dry, or bisque pottery, changing the fired color of the clay body.

Metallic oxide washes are suspended in water and applied to exposed clay. Metallic coloring oxides can be in the form of pencils, crayons, or water-soluble disks of dry pigments.

In the raku firing process, metallic coloring oxides are brushed on a bisque surface, heated, and then subjected to a reduction atmosphere when removed from the kiln. The metallic coloring oxides bond to the clay surface and produce various colors. Copper, as one of the most reactive oxides, can create gold, red, yellow, orange, purple, and blue flashing in reduction conditions.

Metallic oxide/stain fuming: Brush a kiln post or refractory surface with a paint-consistency mixture of oxide, carbonate, or stain. Then place the post close to the clay body or glaze surface. At temperature, the color fumes, or vaporizes, off the refractory painted surface and onto the clay surface, leaving a "blush," or vapor trail, of color. The pattern and color of the fume is dependent on the temperature at which the coloring agent volatizes, the shape of the refractory surface, the shape of the pot, the fuming agent, and the kiln atmosphere.

Metallic salt fuming/metallic lusters: Introduce fuming salts of tin chloride and bismuth sub-nitrate to the kiln during its cooling cycle, at approximately 1,292°F (700°C). Add strontium nitrate and barium chloride to tin chloride to produce red and blue lusters. As the salts volatilize, they land on exposed clay body surfaces. The pattern and area of coverage depends on the amount of salts introduced (100 grams per 40 cubic feet (1.1 m³) of interior kiln space is a workable ratio of salt to kiln space) and the point of entry. The salts can produce a thin, easily abraded, dull pearl-like iridescence on exposed clay body surfaces. The fuming effects on the fired clay look very much like oil on a water

Metallic Fuming Colors	
Blue	**Grams**
Stannous chloride	7
Strontium nitrate	2
Barium cloride	4
Red	
Stannous chloride	16
Strontium nitrate	2
Barium cloride	1
Pearl	
Stannous chloride	7
Bismouth subnitrate	3

surface. Vapors from metallic salt fuming are toxic. Use the correct respirator filter in a well-ventilated studio.

Or, try using gold and silver metallic lusters in an oil base. Apply a thin coat to the clay surface. Lusters also can be applied directly to an unglazed surface by brushing, spraying, sponging, or other application methods. Fire to cone 022 (1,087°F [586°C]). At this point, the oil base is driven off, leaving a thin layer of metal that fuses with the underlying clay body. You can formulate luster colors or purchase them from a ceramics supplier.

Clay Slips (engobes): Slips can contribute color to a clay body surface; in fact, they are essentially colored clays. Slips contain water, clay(s), and other ceramic materials that adhere to a leather-hard or bisque clay body when brushed, dipped, or sprayed. Color the slip by adding metallic coloring oxides, metallic coloring carbonates, or stains. Although there is not enough glass formulation in the slip to result in a fired glaze surface, the slip will fuse to the underlying clay body and alter its color.

Terra sigillata: The Latin term *terra sigillata* means "sealed earth," and it is derived from a specific platelet size liquid clay, which is spread thinly on a leather-hard pot. After the terra sigillata coating dries out, it can be burnished to align the clay platelets parallel to the underlying clay body. When the terra sigillata surface is fired, it fuses slightly, causing a smooth, satin-colored clay surface. Experiment with clay base and metallic coloring oxides or stains to create different terra sigillata effects. As with slips and engobes, a white clay base will showcase colored additives.

Glaze Flashing: Change in clay body color can occur on the exposed clay edge of a glaze-fired surface. Salts contained in glaze migrate out into the clay body during firing, resulting in darker clay flashing along the clay/glaze line. A darker brown vapor line is prevalent when iron exists in the clay body and it is fluxed by the soluble salt migration from the glaze. The line of discoloration on the clay body can extend ¼ to ½ inch (6 to 13 mm) past the glaze line.

A chrome oxide wash (left) is painted on the clay body and is deposited in the recessed areas. A black stain, mason #6600, (right) is applied using the same technique.

The refractory tile (left) is painted with cobalt oxide and fired next to an unglazed clay surface.

> ### TIP
> ## Glass Formation
> Increasing the firing temperature of a clay body will produce additional glass formation within the clay. Any iron, manganese, or metallic coloring oxides found in the clay will cause the clay body to darken in the fired color as metallic coloring oxides flux.

Ceramics Showcase: Special Glaze Effects

This ceramic piece features blue slip trailing; it was fired in an oxidation atmosphere at cone 6 (2,232°F [1,222°C]).

A fishing lure with a metallic luster surface. Metallic lusters can be applied to a fired glaze surface. When fired at a lower temperature, the luster fuses to the underlying glaze surface.

Terra sigillata fired in an oxidation kiln atmosphere at cone 08 (1,728°F [942°C]). Artist: Richard Buncamper

Glaze fuming on to the clay body. Some glaze goes through a period during firing during which vapor is released from the melting surface and can land on exposed clay surfaces. Artist: Emily Pearlman

TROUBLESHOOTING S-CRACK ISSUES

At some point, every amateur or professional potter is disappointed and humbled by the sight of a crack in a favorite pot. Clay can fracture at any time during the forming, drying, or firing stages. There are several different types of cracks, all of which are preventable—most of the time. Identifying the type of crack is the first step in finding the cause and subsequent correction.

An S crack is one of the most common clay defects in wheel work. Understanding the configuration on how clay platelets are aligned in the centering and cone pulling up operation is essential to developing the techniques to prevent S cracks.

An "S" on the bottom of a piece of wheel-thrown pottery. The crack can reveal itself in the forming, drying, bisque, or glaze firing stages. The defect is caused by improper cone pulling up techniques before the clay is centered on the potter's wheel.

The Distinct S-Crack Shape

As the name implies, the crack is shaped like the letter S. They are found at the bottom of pots. S cracks develop during the forming stages of the pot on the wheel and appear in the drying, bisque-firing, or glaze-firing stages. As the pot dries (dry shrinkage) and during the bisque and glaze firing (fired shrinkage), the ware shrinks, causing the crack to fully develop and become visible. When a pot has been glazed, an S crack will appear with a round edge.

S cracks are formed in the initial stages of the throwing operation and can be eliminated by properly bringing the clay up into a cone shape on the wheel.

TIP

S-Crack Qualities

Why did the S crack form? Find out by determining whether the S crack is a round-edge crack or a sharp-edge crack.

Round-edge cracks generally are covered with glaze and have rounded borders where the fired-glaze surface rolls back from the edge. These cracks are caused in the drying, forming, or bisque-firing stages before glaze is applied to the pot.

Cracks that have a sharp, hairline edge on a fired-glazed surface are cooling cracks. These occur after the liquid glaze has set or hardened on the pot.

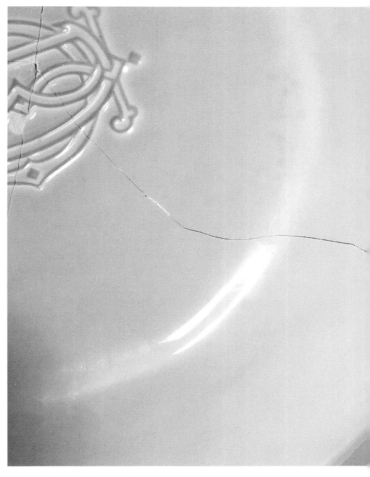

Sharp-edge cooling crack.

Comparison of Clay and Glaze Cracks

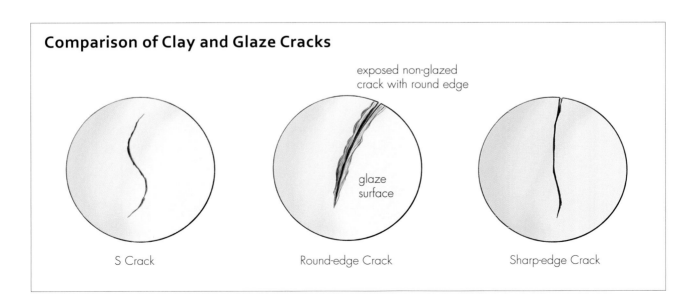

exposed non-glazed crack with round edge

glaze surface

S Crack   Round-edge Crack   Sharp-edge Crack

S-Crack Formation

S cracks can occur on the inside or outside bottoms of wheel-thrown forms. Wider-based forms, such as plates, have a greater chance of producing S cracks. These cracks also occur in forms thrown "off the hump." (A hump is a large piece of clay from which small objects such as tea bowls are formed. The form is cut off and the next pot is formed from some of the remaining mound of clay.) S cracks also result from incorrect technique before pulling up the thrown form.

Now, let's examine the dynamics of S-crack formation. Clay bodies consist of numerous clay platelets that are held together by thin films of water. This unique bonding structure gives moist clay its plastic quality. S cracks can develop when clay platelets in the base of the pot are not aligned in concentric rings (see diagram). The crack forms when the base of the pot and its wall structure have different rates of shrinkage in the drying stage.

To correct S cracks, the clay platelets in the base of the pot must be aligned with the direction of the spinning wheel. This way, the base and walls of the pot have equal shrinkage rates.

 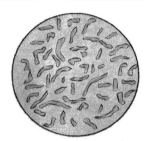

Diagram A: Clay platelets are correctly aligned in concentric rings, which will prevent an S crack from forming.

Diagram B: Clay platelets are not aligned in concentric rings; this could result in an S crack.

Five Steps to Prevent S-Cracks

Prevent S cracks by pulling up clay into a cone shape and then pushing it down before the actual centering takes place in the throwing operation. Pulling the clay up into a cone, if executed properly, will prevent S cracks.

Note: The following directions apply to right-handed potters.

Equipment

- Moist clay

Instructions

① Make sure the left hand is positioned straight up at a right angle to the bat before pushing in toward the center. Apply equal pressure down with the right palm and in with the left hand, pushing the clay toward the center of the bat. Be sure to use water to lubricate the centering clay. During this process, rest your elbows on your knees or brace them close to your body to gain stability and improve leverage.

② As the wheel is turning, apply equal pressure inward with both hands to bring up the clay The compression will cause a convex "nipple" of clay to form at the top.

③ At this stage, the form should look more like a cylinder than a pyramid. When the form is complete, it should have a slightly wider base.

④ Sometimes, the form can take on a "mushroom" shape as it is pressed downward. Correct this by increasing the pressure with the left hand, pushing toward the center as the wheel spins.

⑤ Now consider the height and width of the object you will throw. Horizontal forms, such as plates, will start with a wider base than narrow forms, such as cups.

① Center the clay.

② Pull up the cone.

③ Create the cone shape.

④ Push down the cone.

⑤ Determine a shape.

Incorrect Coning Technique

Improper technique when centering and coning clay on the wheel can allow S cracks to form in moist clay. There are several situations to avoid when pulling up the clay into a cone shape. Often, potters are discouraged when they attempt the cone-up procedure, only to eventually see an S crack appear in their ware in the leather-hard, bone-dry, bisque, or glaze-firing stages. At this point, review the cone-up procedure. This process is almost always the origin of an S crack.

First, when bringing the clay up into a cone shape, keep the base of the cone narrow. A wide base will defeat the purpose of the cone-up procedure. The correct cone procedure produces a form more like a cylinder (see photo A) than a pyramid shape (see photo B).

If the top of the cone develops a recessed or concave area (see photo C), the clay platelets are not aligned correctly. In many instances, an S crack is already in place when the cone is pushed down and the clay is finally centered on the wheel head. To prevent the defect, apply equal pressure with your index fingers and thumbs when arriving at the upper part of the cone (see photo D). The top part of the cone should never have a recessed area at any stage when bringing the clay up into a cone or pushing it down for the centering operation.

If the clay platelets are not aligned properly, there is a greater chance of an S crack forming because of centering technique and clay body formula. When using the correct cone-forming technique, a circular alignment of the clay body platelets helps prevent S cracks.

B. Incorrect cone shape

C. Incorrect concave shape

A. Correct cone shape

D. Correct convex shape

Wheel-thrown Bottle by Joel Harley
9 ½" (24.1 cm) tall, 6 ½" (16.5 cm) diameter
Firing: cone 04 (1,945°F [1,063°C]), oxidation atmosphere (electric kiln)
See formula on page 162

APPENDIX I:
Going into the Ceramics Business

The ability to sell what you make is seductive, and most potters will at some point face the question of when and how to sell their work. However, without a thorough knowledge of business practices, selling pottery can lead to a loss of money and time. Business people who become potters make money; potters who try to become businesspeople lose money. Business training makes all the difference.

At first, selling is easy. Relatives and close friends buy your goods, but before long, they will exhaust their need for pottery. Meanwhile, the pottery market has low barriers to entry: Expenses for starting the business are modest, and many potters sell their work with little initial effort. The initial influx of income from an immediate circle of supporters to cover equipment and supplies often is misleading.

To sell profitably requires developing skills necessary to run a business that just happens to focus on pottery. You must have an extensive knowledge of the market in which you hope to sell pottery. Handmade functional pottery competes with mass-marketed and mass-produced commercial pottery. You must ask yourself: How many people within a limited geographic market will buy a relatively expensive handmade piece instead of an inexpensive machine-made cup?

Plan Your Business

Some potters' long-range plans consist of packing the car up for the next craft show. Whether the expense of going to the show will justify the anticipated revenues is often overlooked. Develop real plans for marketing and advertising your work that are based on research. Your plan should include an evaluation of prospective craft shows, a timetable to reach short- and long-term goals, and a listing of primary and secondary markets for your pots. The plan should also include a complete financial breakdown of direct and indirect costs of production, hourly wages for yourself, and profit margins. Committing your ideas to paper in the form of a business plan allows you to prioritize your goals. For example, projecting revenues for particular pottery shows allows you to establish production goals.

Keep accurate, up-to-date financial records so you can spot the first indications of business difficulty. Be sure to calculate fixed and variable costs so you can establish a wholesale and retail pricing structure. Fixed costs include studio insurance, rent or mortgage payments, heating and lighting costs, and any other recurring costs to do business. Variable costs include materials and supplies to produce pots, supplies for stationary, and studio clean-up materials.

In addition to keeping financial and inventory records, you will record the results of glaze tests and kiln firings so you can duplicate good results and continue to improve efficiency and, ultimately, profit margin. Develop numbering systems and file test-tile results so you can refer to them without sifting through a messy studio.

A Pottery Business Plan

A comprehensive business plan for your pottery should include the following topics.

Description of the product: What kind of pottery will be produced?

Marketing of the product: How will the company promote, distribute, and sell the pottery?

Financing of the company: Will personal savings fund start-up costs and operating expenses, or will you seek outside financing?

Management of the company: Will the business be staffed by a sole proprietor, or will you employ others?

Ask yourself the following questions as you develop a business plan.

What exactly is the market? Who will buy my pottery? What is their income range, education, history of buying pottery, and reasons for pottery buying?

Where are the customers? Do they live in-state, out-of-state, in the city, or country?

What are the customers' buying patterns? Do they buy pottery every week, month, year? Do they buy through craft shows, galleries, the Internet, catalogs, direct from potters?

Why should they buy pottery from my company? List specific value-added features in pottery, such as unique glaze colors, durability, ease of use, and wide assortments of functional pottery.

Should I concentrate on the whole market or a segment? Should I try to sell pottery to everyone or to potential customers who are craft-oriented?

What is the competition? Are other potters making similar pottery? Are pottery imports a larger part of the market?

What are the competition's strengths and weaknesses? Examples: The competition produces equal- or superior-quality pottery. However, the competition does not make custom pottery.

How can I improve my product over the competition? Should I use unique glazes? Should I specialize in making pottery sets? Should I customize the pottery with slogans or names of customers?

Is the market stable, growing, shrinking? Are people buying more pots this year than in the past five, ten, or fifteen years? What is the projected growth of the handmade-pottery market?

What is my plan for growing the business? I plan to advertise in a local newspaper. I plan on hiring studio help to increase production. I intend to send literature to past customers notifying them of future pottery sales.

There is a great deal more to learn about running a pottery business; we've given the topic an extreme overview. Check into business classes and workshops at local community colleges and ask other professional potters to share their successes and failures. The more you educate yourself about the business of your pottery, the better you will fare when selling your work.

Plan Your Production Time

Making pottery is a demanding, labor-intensive, and repetitive activity. It can be doubly harsh if you don't like the actual pots you are making. Design and formulate pots that are fun to turn out. Then search for a suitable market, so they will sell. Succumbing to trends (such as a popular glaze color) might produce short-term results but may eventually make potting a dull job. Many potters compromise and produce objects they know will sell, even though the pottery might be less than interesting to produce. Once the "guaranteed-income pots" are finished, they create the work they enjoy. If you choose this path, maintain a balance between the "paycheck pots" and those that express your aesthetic statement and beliefs.

As you strike a balance, be sure to set limits. Pottery making requires planning, execution, and evaluation of the outcome. Time is your most important commodity, and your greatest business expense. Calculate your time carefully, and don't underestimate the time invested in all stages of production.

Avoid the following common time traps.

Don't make custom individual pots to order. Turning down a request for a personalized plate or bowl is often difficult, but almost every potter has been placed in this situation by family, friends, and customers. It can easily turn into a time and cost trap. If custom work is needed, first show samples of what the customer can expect and don't stray from the sample options in fulfilling the order.

Don't make replacements to a set you no longer produce, and do not make a replacement for a set by another potter. Changes in raw materials, firing cycles, glazing techniques, and other variables make it difficult to reproduce a pot precisely to match other pieces you made in the past. Consider making extra pieces in a set during the original production run. While storage and handling of the extra pots may be a problem, future time and effort is saved.

Plan Your Purchases and Pricing

Keep your clay body and glaze formulas simple by using as few raw materials as possible. Many basic versions of clay body and glaze formulas produce the same fired effect as formulas containing numerous raw materials. Fewer raw materials in the studio translates to easier and faster weigh-outs of glaze or clay body formulas. It also simplifies ordering.

Make buying decisions with care. Research moist clays, tools, equipment, and raw materials before committing to a ceramics supplier. Before choosing a supplier, decide if you need a full-service supplier, with a store location displaying equipment, tools, books, supplies, and a sales staff, or a discount ceramics supplier, which might not have a store or an extensive selection but offers competitive pricing. Always inquire about return policies. Also, ask other potters about their experiences with specific suppliers.

When pricing your pots, figure in all production costs, including hourly wage and profit margin at every stage. Cut costs where possible, but think how a cost reduction can impact the whole system. One potter decided to eliminate the bisque-firing process, thereby saving time and fuel costs. However, he did not adjust the glaze formulas for raw glazing and single firing. Several glazes peeled off of the wares during glaze-firing, and he lost many pots.

Marketing Your Pottery

Venues for pottery sales range from going to craft fairs to selling directly from your studio. Consider the following factors when deciding where to sell pottery: cost structure, location, personal contacts, individual style of pottery, and supplemental income.

Wheel-thrown jar with cover.

Creative Marketing

One potter traveled to several local nurseries that sell miniature trees (Bonsai plants) and sold planters to the stores. Planned diversification of sales outlets will ensure the best chance of future sales. However, too many marginal venues can lead to loss of product or no income for the effort of shipping and stocking.

You may sell your pottery in one venue—art shows or craft fairs, for example—or you may diversify by targeting several of the following outlets. Through trial and error (and hopefully, some number-crunching and strategy on your part), you'll discover which sales avenues produce the highest profit margins and income.

The Studio Gallery

Selling directly from your studio offers several benefits. First, customers are attracted to the idea of purchasing a pot hot from the kiln. You can even notify customers about your firing schedule. Packing and shipping costs are avoided, and there's no risk of breakage during transport. (This is a concern when traveling to craft shows, for instance.) Ideally, your studio should be located in an area with lots of foot traffic, and attractive display windows are important. Otherwise, shoppers will not know what's going on inside.

Craft Shows

Craft shows can generate fast income compared to other selling methods, such as waiting for customers to buy your pots from a gallery or retail store. Some craft shows are structured to sell wholesale and retail. Buyers from retail stores and art galleries are invited into the show the first day or two, after which the general public is admitted. Wholesale selling presents a different set of challenges to the potter and should be carefully investigated. (We'll talk more about wholesale selling on page 149.)

Regardless of your pricing, an inviting booth is the most important tool for increasing sales. Display business cards and post photographs of your work. Customers may wish to contact you after the show to make a purchase. To take advantage of high foot traffic, provide a sign-up book for customers to leave their names, street addresses, and email addresses. Use this later to market your work through post cards or email announcements.

Galleries selling to the public either acquire pottery on consignment or purchase pots directly from the potter for retail sales.

Consignment Sales

A gallery or retail store will exhibit your pottery on consignment: you give the store free inventory and you will receive payment when the pottery is sold. This type of sales has several negatives. The store and the potter have to keep exact records of transactions. Often, tracking the sale of pottery, restocking pottery, and the payment are time-consuming repetitive efforts. The potter must rely on the store's personnel to maintain and exhibit the pottery without loss or neglect. Finally, pottery on consignment is not available for sale in other venues in which money collection is immediate.

Wholesale Opportunities

You can sell pottery wholesale through art/craft galleries, retail stores, craft shows, or catalogs. Investigate the reputation of the seller before signing any business contract. The first sale of pottery should be for cash-on-delivery or a prepaid order. Generally, the wholesale price of pottery is one-half the retail price, but this percentage can vary. Decide on some ratio of wholesale-to-retail sales to ensure a consistent revenue source.

Always look for new wholesale markets and develop relationships with buyers. This applies to one-time retail sales, wholesale selling, or pottery exhibited to sell in galleries. Consider enlisting a representative (a friend with a marketing brain or a polite family member).

Before committing to any venue, make sure you can meet any eventual demand for the pottery. A potter may be pleased when his work is highlighted in a catalog, but can be ill-equipped when a high volume of orders is generated.

Internet Sales

Traditionally, Internet sales of pottery have not produced a high level of income for potters. The best use of the Web has been to lead people to a potter's studio or store where the pottery is being sold. Most customers want to handle pots before committing to a purchase. That said, the Internet is an invaluable marketing tool today, and a professional-looking website will attract customers who are serious about buying quality pottery. The most productive websites feature professionally photographed, clear images and well written, descriptive text of the pottery. If sales originate from the studio, a detailed map listing hours of operation and directions will lead customers easily to your pottery shop. List retail store and gallery locations, along with customer testimonials.

Pottery on display represents functional and sculptural work by professional potters.

Creating Functional Sets to Sell

A complete set of dinner plates, lunch plates, cups, bowls, pitchers, and other forms is enticing for prospective customers. In many instances, customers do not intend to buy sets until they see the display. When customers are faced with grouping individual pots to form a set, they may be overwhelmed and, instead, will purchase nothing at all. Make the buying decision easy by creating and displaying sets of various glaze colors, sizes, and details.

A set can be similar in size, glaze-color combination, or forming technique.

What Is a Set?

A set can consist of any number of pottery forms. To create a set, choose the defining characteristics of the group. Will all the bowls be the same size, shape, or glaze color? Will all pieces have the same surface design elements and clay body color?

The next question is how many pieces comprise a set. A set should be apparent to others when in use or on display. Simply put, when customers enter a pottery display booth or visit a studio, they should recognize without question that a designated group of pottery objects is a set.

An important but simple rule to consider is that functional objects need to function. Bowls should hold liquids and solids, stack easily in the cupboard, be easily cleaned, and generally fit into the kitchen workspace. A pitcher should pour liquid without dribbling down its spout. The lids of covered jars should fit properly. Before creating sets, make several prototype pieces and use them in your own kitchen for a trial run. Tweak your design, if necessary, then begin creating the sets.

Sets should have a common design element that unifies them visually and/or structurally. All of the pieces don't have to be exactly alike, but they should be similar on some level. Just as human beings are unique, handmade pottery sets should reflect that intrinsic aspect of their production.

Creating a Set

Usually, the first few pots in a set are "stiff" and self-conscious in form, while succeeding pots becoming more fluid and confident in structure. After several kiln loads or production cycles, you'll begin to make improved editions of individual pieces within the set.

Equipment
- Moist clay
- Scale

Instructions

① Weigh out a fixed amount of clay for each pot in the set. This ensures a degree of uniformity in all pots. For instance, if you weigh out four 1-pound (454-g) pieces of clay, you will throw four coffee cups close in size. Apply the same weighing technique to hand building to duplicate the scale of an object. This is your first step toward standardizing the clay form. Also, each piece of clay should contain the same moisture content to achieve consistency in the forming process. The main idea in producing sets is to eliminate as many variables as possible, so you can concentrate on making each piece similar.

② Think functional. While some degree of random qualities or handmade features are a definite promotional point in functional pottery, selling items to the public requires a number of basic constraints as to the size and shape of the pottery. For example, it would not improve the selling qualities of plates if they could not fit into a standard dishwasher or kitchen cabinet. Likewise, dinner plates with deep recessed throwing ridges may appear attractive, but plates without a flat surface on which to cut food are not functional. The general public is interested in handmade products, but they don't want to spend extra time washing or alter the way they would typically use a plate to accommodate "artistic license."

③ Make a set during one sitting. Repetition yields efficiency. On the wheel, most functional pottery can be thrown within a few minutes of starting to form the clay. Making a set of six cups within one working session should be possible. The average time to throw a small cup should be one to two minutes. If you throw one or two cups but wait until later in the day or the following week to finish, they'll be inconsistent.

④ Make a series of the same form. Series also qualify as sets. A series can denote a slight but intentional change in each piece. The evolution can be in shape, scale, glaze, or pattern. A wheel-thrown cylinder shape offers an excellent example of one way to think about series. Starting from 1/2-pound (227-g) balls of clay, you can form small cylinders to make teacups, coffee cups, and small vases. The same procedures can be applied to creating a set or series of nesting bowls, just by increasing the amount of clay used to make the same bowl shape in varying sizes.

⑤ Experiment with glaze techniques. It is often easier to try various glaze patterns or glaze colors on similar forms. Working from a standard object (similar pots or sculpture pieces in a set or series), apply glazes in numerous patterns. For example, glaze one piece blue, another yellow, the next green, and so on. It is usually most productive to choose one type of form and work out the glazing techniques either through repetition or slight variations.

⑥ Stack pots in a set to best use kiln space. Because all of the pieces in the set will be the same, or at least have some common design elements, stacking the pots in a bisque or a glaze kiln allows the wares to fit in limited kiln space more efficiently. In the bisque kiln, save space by placing nesting bowls within each other. In the glaze kiln, place cylinder sets very close to each other, using every part of the kiln shelf. Denser stacking of the bisque and glaze kilns translates into more pots per cubic foot of kiln space, greatly reducing fuel costs.

TIP
Make Extra

Always turn out more pieces than required to complete a set. Making additional pieces will ensure at least some will come through the pottery-making process without defects. It will also allow for choosing the best pieces to form the set. The extra time and effort required to produce the work is nothing compared with the disappointment of not being able to assemble a complete set.

A set should feature pieces that are relatively similar in theme, such as glaze color, size, or form.

Limited Editions

A limited edition is a finite number of prints made from a single printing plate. People love to collect, and if the collectable has a rare or limited quality to it, all the better. For example, produce a series of thirty platters. Sign each platter with the date it was produced and the edition number (15/30, for example, indicates it was the fifteenth platter made out of a total edition of thirty platters). This adds value to each platter sold. Your next series of editions could be cups or covered jars.

Making limited editions is a simple but effective method for making sets and still selling individual pieces. Similarly, you can make a theme or motif a design element, such as a tree pattern in the glaze or a calligraphy pattern on pitchers. While both marketing techniques might sound too commercial, remember that the challenge is to introduce your aesthetic to the selling environment. Your potter's signature or mark on each piece further identifies the work as an object made by an individual craftsman and not a machine. Increase your sales by signing all of your work, and make a point of showing customers your signature.

The potter's signature on the pots is a handmade statement that mass-produced factory-made pottery cannot rival.

APPENDIX II:
Clay and Glaze Formulas

Potters often ask about other potters' work, "How did they make that?" The clay and glaze formulas here are yours to enjoy and experiment with. Clay body formulas, glaze formulas, forming, and firing methods often give insight into how potters accomplish their aesthetic goals. The technical aspects behind a piece can jumpstart your own work, but formulas alone are not the final arbiter of quality. Good pots are more than the sum of their parts. They are the result of experience, trial and error, practice, and persistence.

Because the formulations for clay and glaze components change over time, always test clay bodies and glazes to ensure an accurate result.

The glaze formulas and clay body formulas are listed in percentages. This allows potters to generate batches of material in any quantity desired. G-200 feldspar at 45 percent can be used as 45 grams, 450 grams, or 4,500 grams, as long as the other materials in the formula are increased by the same factor. The base clay body and glaze components total 100 percent, and coloring oxides, stains, grogs, gums, and other additives are added beyond 100 percent.

Thrown Cylinder

7" (17.8 cm) tall, 3" (7.6 cm) diameter
Firing: Cone 9 (2,300°F [1,260°C]), reduction atmosphere

Clay Body Color: Brown/Stoneware	%
A.P.G. Missouri fireclay 35x	25
Goldart stoneware clay	41
Thomas ball clay	15
Custer feldspar (potassium)	12
Flint 200x	7
Grog 48/f	6

Glaze Color: Matte Yellow

	%
G-200 feldspar (potassium)	45
Flint 325x	5
E.P.K.	25
Dolomite	22
Whiting	3

Glaze Color: Matte Red

	%
G-200 feldspar (potassium)	48
E.P.K.	21
Dolomite	13
Whiting	8
Tin oxide	4
Bone ash (natural)	6
Red iron oxide	4

Thrown Jar

7 1/2" (19.1 cm) tall, 10" (25.4 cm) diameter
Firing: Unglazed, cone 01 (2,046°F [1,119°C]), oxidation atmosphere (electric kiln)

Clay Body: Black	%
Goldart stoneware clay	34
Pine Lake fireclay	20
Tennessee ball clay #1	16
Nepheline syenite 270x (sodium)	16
Flint 200x	10
Redart earthenware clay	4
Grog 80x	6
Cobalt oxide	1 1/2

Square-Sided Thrown Raku Covered Jar

14" (35.6 cm) tall, 3 ³/₄" (9.5 cm) diameter
Firing: cone 04 (1,945°F [1,063°C]), reduction atmosphere

Clay Body: Gray/Black/Raku	%
Goldart stoneware	50
Tennessee ball clay #1	15
Pine Lake Fireclay	18
A.P.G. fireclay 28x	5
Custer feldspar (potassium)	7
Flint 200x	5
Grog 48/f	7

Glaze: Opaque White

Gerstley borate	36
Custer feldspar (potassium)	32
E.P.K.	2
Flint 325x	30
Superpax	12

Wheel-Thrown Altered Oval

3¹/₂" (8.9 cm) tall, 7 ¹/₄ " (18.4 cm) wide
Firing cone 10 (2,345°F [1,285°C]), reduction atmosphere

Clay Body: Brown/Stoneware	%
Hawthorn Bond fireclay 50x	21
Goldart stoneware clay	50
Kentucky ball clay OM#4	15
Custer feldspar (potassium)	8
Flint 200x	6
Grog 48/f	8

Glaze: Gloss Red

Custer feldspar (potassium)	57
Whiting	20
Ferro frit #3134	6
Flint 325x	15
Tin oxide	2
Copper carbonate	2¹/₂

Wheel-Thrown Unglazed Bowl

7" (17.8 cm) tall, 7 ½" (19.1 cm) diameter
Firing: cone 04 (1,945°F [1,063°C]) oxidation atmosphere
(electric kiln)

Clay Body: White/Earthenware	%
Tennessee ball clay #1	47
Texas talc	50
Whiting	3
Wash: Brown/Black	
Red iron oxide	40
Rutile powdered lt.	40
Ferro frit #3195	20

Wheel-Thrown/Hand-Built Sculptural Disk

11" (27.9 cm) tall, 12" (30.5 cm) diameter
Firing: cone 9 (2,300°F [1,260°C]) reduction atmosphere,
unglazed

Clay Body: Black/Stoneware	%
Goldart stoneware clay	38
Pine Lake fireclay	20
Tennessee ball clay #1	15
Nepheline syenite 270x (sodium)	12
Flint 200x	7
Redart earthenware clay	8
Grog 80x	14
Cobalt oxide	1 ½
Red iron oxide	1

Clay Body: Brown/Stoneware	%
Goldart stoneware clay	25
Pine Lake fireclay	33
Tennessee ball clay #1	10
Nepheline syenite 270x (sodium)	20
Flint 200x	8
Redart earthenware clay	4
Grog 80x	12
Glaze: Satin Matte Green	
Cornwall stone	46
Whiting	34
E.P.K.	20
Copper carbonate	4
Tin oxide	4

Slab Construction Oval Platter
Artist: Jim Fineman

1" (2.5 cm) tall, 10¼" (26 cm) diameter
Firing: cone 9 (2,300°F [1,260°C]), reduction atmosphere

Wheel-Thrown Bottle

9" (22.9 cm) tall, 4" (10.2 cm) diameter
Firing: cone 9 (2,300°F [1,260°C]), reduction atmosphere

Clay Body: Brown/Red Stoneware	%
Hawthorn Bond fireclay 50x	30
Goldart stoneware	35
Thomas ball clay	12
Newman red stoneware	10
Custer feldspar (potassium)	8
Flint 200x	5
Grog Ohio #3 40/f	12

Glaze: Gloss Brown/White	
Nepheline syenite 270x (sodium)	47
Soda ash	13
E.P.K.	15
F-4 feldspar (sodium)	10
Thomas ball clay	10
Redart earthenware clay	5

Wheel-Thrown Disk

2 1/2" (5.7 cm) tall, 9" (22.9 cm) wide
Firing: cone 04 (1,945°F [1,063°C]), oxidation atmosphere (electric kiln)

Clay Body: Light Brown/Earthenware	%
Redart	85
Thomas ball clay	15
Barium carbonate	0.3

White Slip	
E.P.K.	25
Pioneer kaolin	15
Tennessee ball clay #10	10
Nepheline syenite 270x (sodium)	15
Flint 325x	10
Superpax	10
Soda ash	5
Ferro frit #3110	10

Wheel-Thrown Bowl

6 ¹/₂″ (16.5 cm) tall, 7 ¹/₂″ (19.1 cm) diameter
Firing: cone 10 (2,345°F [1,285°C]) soda firing

Clay Body: Brown/Stoneware	%
Grolleg kaolin	25
A.P.G. Missouri fire clay 28x	25
Goldart stoneware clay	30
Tennessee ball clay #9	10
XX sagger clay	5
Custer feldspar (potassium)	5
Silica sand F-65 48x	4
Grog 48/f	4

Glaze: Green Gloss

Albany slip	80
Whiting	20

White Slip

E.P.K	35
Flint 325x	20
Tennessee ball clay #1	15
Superpax	5
Cornwall stone	25

Wheel-Thrown Oval Cylinder
Artist: Tom White

8 ¹/₂″ (21.6 cm) tall, 5″ (12.7 cm) wide
Firing: cone 11 (2,361°F [1,294°C]) wood/soda/salt

Clay Body: Light Medium Brown/Stoneware	%
Hawthorn Bond fireclay 50x	33
Goldart stoneware	24
Lizella stoneware	10
Tennessee ball clay #9	12
Custer feldspar (potassium)	13
Flint 200x	8
Silica sand F-65 48x	12

Glaze: Gloss White

Custer feldspar (potassium)	30
Nepheline syenite 270x (sodium)	39
Soda ash	8
Tennessee ball clay #1	17
E.P.K.	6

White Slip

Helmer kaolin	65
Grolleg kaolin	20
Nepheline syenite 270x (sodium)	15

Wheel-Thrown Covered Jar
Artist: Tom White

5$\frac{1}{2}$" (14 cm) tall, 5$\frac{1}{2}$" (14.6 cm) diameter
Firing: cone 11 (2,361°F [1,294°C]) reduction atmosphere
(soda firing)

Clay Body: Medium Brown/Stoneware	%
Hawthorn Bond fireclay 50x	20
Goldart stoneware clay	40
Kentucky ball clay OM#4	15
G-200 feldspar (potassium)	12
Flint 200x	8
Redart earthenware clay	5
Grog 20/48x	12

Glaze: Gloss Light Green with White Stripes	
Custer feldspar (potassium)	28
Flint 325x	34
E.P.K.	2
Talc	4
Whiting	18
Barium carbonate	12
Bone ash (natural)	2
Copper carbonate	2

White Overglaze	
Custer feldspar (potassium)	49
E.P.K.	21
Dolomite	19
Whiting	4
Tin oxide	7

Wheel-Thrown Bowl
Artist: Tom White

2$\frac{1}{2}$" (7 cm) tall, 4" (10.2 cm) diameter
Firing: cone 6 (2,232°F [1,222°C]) reduction wood
firing then cone 10 (2,345°F [1,285°C]) soda firing

Clay Body: White/Stoneware	%
Cedar Heights bonding clay 50x	22
Goldart stoneware clays	19
Hawthorn Bond fire clay 35x	21
Tennessee ball clay #10	13
XX sagger clay	10
Flint 200x	9
Custer feldspar (potassium)	6
Silica sand F-95 70x	9

Glaze: Gloss White	
Custer feldspar (potassium)	49
E.P.K.	21
Dolomite	19
Whiting	4
Tin oxide	7

Wheel-Thrown Goblet

7 1/2" (19.7 cm) tall, 5" (12.7 cm) diameter
Firing: cone 10 (2,345°F [1,285°C]), soda firing

Wheel-Thrown Covered Jar

7" (17.8 cm) tall, 8" (20.3 cm) diameter
Firing: cone 10 (2,345°F [1,285°C]), reduction atmosphere

Clay Body: White/Porcelain	%
Grolleg kaoliin	50
Custer feldspar (potassium)	25
Flint 200x	25
Silica sand F-95 70x	8

Glaze: Gloss Brown

	%
Albany slip	75
Whiting	20
Flint 325x	5

Green Slip

	%
E.P.K.	35
Grolleg	40
Nepheline syenite 270x (sodium)	15
Ferro frit #3110	5
Flint 325x	5
Copper carbonate	2

Clay Body: Brown/Stoneware	%
A.P.G. Missouri fireclay 28x	21
Goldart stoneware clay	44
Tennessee ball clay #9	16
G-200 feldspar (potassium)	12
Flint 200x	7
Grog 48/f	12

Glaze: Matte Blue/Gray

	%
Custer feldspar (potassium)	45
Flint 325x	5
E.P.K.	25
Dolomite	22
Whiting	3
Cobalt carbonate	1/2
Nickel carbonate green	1

Glaze: Matte Pink

	%
Custer feldspar (potassium)	45
Flint 325x	5
E.P.K.	25
Dolomite	22
Whiting	3
Copper oxide (red)	1/2

Wheel-Thrown Bottle
Artist: Joel Huntley

9¹/₂" (24.1 cm) tall, 6 ¹/₂" (16.5 cm) diameter
Firing: cone 04 (1,945°F [1,063°C]), oxidation atmosphere
(electric kiln)

Clay Body: Brown/Earthenware	%
Redart	55
Cedar Heights bonding clay 50x	9
Thomas ball clay	17
M 44 ball clay	7
Custer feldspar (potassium)	6
Goldart stoneware clay	3
Flint 200x	3

Glaze: Clear Transparent Glossy	
Ferro frit #3269	90
E.P.K.	8
Flint 325x	2
Red iron oxide	1
Epsom salts	¹/₂

White Slip	%
E.P.K.	30
Thomas ball clay	25
M44 ball clay	10
Goldart stoneware clay	5
Flint 325x	20
Superpax	10
Bentonite	2

Yellow Slip Variation	
Mason stain Titanium Yellow #6485	10

Dendritic Slip: Brown/Black	
Manganese dioxide powder	20 grams
Water	29 grams
Apple cider vinegar	29 grams
Tobacco	0.75 gram (one cigarette)

Mixing

Mix all ingredients. Break open and add the contents of one cigarette to the dendritic slip (discard the cigarette filter). Age the slip for 24 hours, then place the liquid through a 100x-mesh sieve three times before using. Discard any material left on the 100x-mesh screen. The shelf life of dendritic slip is two weeks. After that the properties of the growing tree patterns rapidly decline.

Application

After the pot has been thrown, hand-built, or otherwise formed, apply the base slip to the moist and leather-hard clay surface as soon as possible to ensure a stronger bond between the slip and clay body. While the base slip is still wet, immediately dip a soft bristle brush in the dendritic slip mixture. Fill the brush with a small amount of the watercolor-consistency dendritic slip, then barely touch the surface of the wet white slip with the brush. The dendritic slip will flow off the brush onto the base slip, leaving a pattern. A tree-like tentacle decoration can be developed by holding the pot on the vertical. Concentric ring patterns can be obtained by applying dendritic slip to horizontal pot surfaces.

Wheel-Thrown Raku-Fired Vase
Artist: Steven Branfman

8" (20.3 cm) tall, 7" (17.8 cm) diameter
Firing: cone 04 (1,945°F [1,063°C]), fired in an oxidation
atmosphere and fast-cooled in a reduction atmosphere

Clay Body: Black/Gray	%
Hawthorn bond fireclay 50x	45
Talc	20
Kentucky ball clay OM#4	15
Goldart stoneware clay	20
Grog 48/f	20

Glaze: White Satin Matte	
Gerstley borate	65
Tennessee ball clay #9	5
Nepheline syenite 270x (sodium)	15
Tin oxide	10
Flint 200x	5

Overglaze wash: Yellow	
Mason stain Naples #6405	60
Ferro frit #3195	40

Overglaze wash: Green	
Mason stain Bermuda #6242	60
Ferro frit #3195	40

Overglaze wash: Red	
Mason stain Crimson #6003	60
Ferro frit #3195	40

Press-Molded Bowl

1 1/2" (3.8 cm) tall, 5 1/2" (14 cm) diameter
Firing: cone 9 (2,300°F [1,260°C]), reduction atmosphere

Clay Body: White Stoneware	%
Tile #6 kaolin	30
Tennessee ball clay #10	30
G-200 feldspar (potassium)	20
Flint 200x	20
Silica sand F-95 79x	8

Glaze: Light Brown/Yellow	
Cornwall stone	50
Whiting	30
Grolleg kaolin	20
Red iron oxide	4

Wheel-Thrown Bowl

7¹/₂" (19.1 cm) tall, 8" (20.3 cm) diameter
Firing: cone 04 (1,945°F [1,063°C])

Clay Body: Red Earthenware	%
Redart earthenware	75
Sheffield earthenware	15
Goldart stoneware	6
C&C ball clay	4

Clay Body: White Earthenware	
C&C ball clay	50
Talc	47
Whiting	3

Wheel-Thrown Sculptural Rattle

5" (12.7 cm) tall, 12¹/₂" (31.1 cm) long
Firing: cone 9 (2,300°F [1,260°C]), salt-fired with red
fiber flocking

Clay Body: Black Stoneware	%
A.P.G. Missouri fireclay 28x	20
Goldart stoneware clay	25
Ocmulgee stoneware clay	15
Kentucky ball clay OM #4	12
F-4 feldspar (sodium)	12
Flint 200x	10
Redart	6
Silica sand F-95 70x	12
Cobalt oxide	2
Red flocking (Cloth fibers sprayed on adhesive surface)	

Wheel-Thrown Jar

8 1/2" (21 cm) tall, 8" (20.3 cm) diameter
Firing: cone 9 (2,300°F [1,260°C]), salt-fired

Clay Body: White Stoneware	%
A.P.G. Missouri fireclay 28x	20
Goldart stoneware	40
Tennessee ball clay #1	18
G-200 feldspar (potassium)	12
Flint 200x	10
Silica sand F-95 70x	10

Blue Wash

Cobalt carbonate	80
Ferro frit #3124	20

Wheel-Thrown Cup

3 1/2" (8.8 cm) tall, 4" (10.2 cm) diameter
Firing: cone 9 (2,300°F [1,260°C]), reduction atmosphere

Clay Body: White Porcelain	%
Tile #6 kaolin	10
E.P.K.	16
Pioneer kaolin	6
Tennessee ball clay #10	25
G-200 feldspar (potassium)	23
Flint 200x	20

Glaze: Dark Brown, Glossy

Custer feldspar (potassium)	52
Flint 325x	24
Whiting	13
E.P.K.	7
Barium carbonate	2
Zinc oxide	2
Bentonite	2
Red iron oxide	8

APPENDIX III:
Glossary

Albany slip – a low-temperature, high-iron content clay mined in the Albany, New York, region of the United States. Commonly used as a glaze in stoneware and salt-glazed pottery.

A.P.G. Missouri fireclay – a coarse, refractory clay formed against seams of coal, lignite, and other impurities. Used in clay bodies for its "tooth," or ability to stand up in the moist clays forming operations

absorption – the amount of moisture taken into a clay body in the fired state

ball clay – secondary clay transported by water from its forming site. A fine-grained particle size results in a very plastic clay.

barium carbonate – an alkaline earth raw material that can be used in glaze to create opacity and influence the color of metallic coloring oxides

bentonite – very plastic clay formed from volcanic ash. Often used in clay body formulas for its plastic properties. Used in glaze formulas for its suspension properties.

bisque firing – a preliminary firing that removes organic material and mechanical and chemical water; forms the clay in preparation for the glaze firing

blister – a gas inclusion in the clay body. Can disrupt a glaze surface and has sharp crater edges.

bloat – ceramic objects that swell or bulge when subjected to heat in a kiln firing

bone ash – calcium phosphate provides a flux in china bodies; contributes to an opalescent luster in glazes

bone-dry – a drying stage when most of the mechanical water is removed from the clay. Clay is fragile at this stage.

brushing – a method of transferring glaze, engobe, or underglaze color to a ceramic form using a brush

calcined – purifying a material by using heat

carbonaceous – carbon-containing materials found in varying amounts in some clays

carpal tunnel syndrome – a wrist, arm, or hand injury caused by repetitive motion; can cause pain, tingling of the hand, and numbness

casting slip – a fluid clay body that can be poured into plaster molds

C&C ball clay – a small-platelet-sized clay that can be used in a clay body for its plastic properties. In glazes, it contributes suspension properties, alumina, and silica.

Cedar Heights bonding clay 50x – a high-temperature plastic stoneware clay used in clay body formulas. A coarser grind of Goldart stoneware clay.

centering – a preliminary technique for forming moist clay into the exact center of the potter's wheel

chemical water – water that is combined with clay and is not driven off until 842°F to 1,112°F (450°C to 600°C)

clay – igneous rock that has been weathered down. Has a platelet structure. Plastic when moist, hard vitreous when fired.

clay body – a combination of clay(s), fluxes, and inherent materials designed to achieve a specific fired color, temperature range, and forming ability

clay mixer – a machine that mixes dry clay and water to achieve a plastic, consistent mass

clay platelet – the microscopic hexagonal shape of clay; length to thickness ratio is approximately 10:1

clay shrinkage – a reduction in the dimension of clay in the drying or firing stages

cobalt carbonate – one of the most potent ceramic colorants; can produce blue in glazes

concave – a structure with a recessed area, such as the arched curve inside of a bowl

cone – a pyrometric cone formulated from ceramic raw materials; will deform at a given temperature over a specific rate of heat increase

coned up – a procedure that brings moist clay up to a cone shape on the potter's wheel to remove potential "S" cracking

convex – curved or rounded out, such as on the exterior of a sphere

copper carbonate – a glaze coloring agent that can produce blues and greens

copper oxide (red) – a glaze coloring agent that can produce blues and greens. Stronger concentration than copper carbonate.

Cornwall stone – a naturally occurring mineral containing sodium, potassium, calcium, silica, alumina, and other trace materials. Can be used in high-temperature glazes as a flux or glass former in conjunction with other materials in the glaze.

crazing – a fine network of lines formed in the fired glaze when it cools under tension in comparison to the underlying clay body

cristobalite – a crystalline, solid material formed in the conversion of silica

Custer feldspar – potassium-dominate feldspar used in a clay body formula for its high-temperature fluxing ability. In glazes, it is a primary high-temperature flux that melts other glaze materials.

damper – a device in the kiln stack that regulates exhaust immersions from the kiln

Darvan #7 – a polyelectrolyte deflocculant used to make casting slip bodies pourable into molds

deflocculant – a compound, usually sodium-based, that disperses the clay platelets in a water system, causing a fluid clay slip

dipping – a method of applying glaze to a ceramic form by submersion into a glaze container

dolomite – a sedimentary mineral containing equal parts calcium and magnesium

earthenware clay – commonly found clays that when fired to low temperatures (1,657° F to 1,945°F [903°C to 1,063°C]) are nonvitreous and porous

electric kiln – a kiln heated by electric coils firing in an oxidation atmosphere

engobe – another term for a decorative slip applied to the ware; a liquid suspension of clay(s) with additional flux and other materials

E.P.K. – Edgar Plastic Kaolin, a refractory primary white firing clay used in clay body and glaze formulas

epsom salts – magnesium sulfate, used in glazes for its suspension properties

ergonomic – tools designed for comfortable handling

eutectic – a mixture of two or more materials that has a lower melting point than any of the original, raw materials

F-4 – a sodium-based feldspar used in a clay body formula for its high-temperature fluxing ability. In glazes, it is a primary, high-temperature flux, bringing other glaze materials into a melt.

feldspar – weathered-down granite that forms an alkaline flux in clay bodies and glazes

ferro frit #3134 – a low-temperature flux combination of sodium, calcium, boron, and silica that has been calcined, ground into a powder, and used in low- to medium-temperature glazes

ferro frit #3195 – a low-temperature flux combination of sodium, calcium, boron, alumina, and silica that has been calcined, ground into a powder, and used in low- to medium-temperature glazes

ferro frit #3110 – a low-temperature flux combination of potassium, sodium, calcium, alumina, boron, and silica that can be used in low- to medium-temperature glazes

ferro frit #3269 – a low-temperature flux combination of potassium, sodium, calcium, zinc, alumina, boron, and silica that can be used in low- to medium-temperature glazes

ferro frit #3124 – a low-temperature flux combination of potassium, sodium, calcium, alumina, boron, and silica used in low- to medium-temperature glazes

filter press – a method of mixing clay and water in which the liquid clay is squeezed between many cloth bags to remove excess water

fireclay – refractory clay with high amounts of alumina and silica

firing – the process of heating pottery in a kiln

flame ware – clay bodies and glazes designed to withstand direct flame impingement from cooking stoves

flint – commonly called silica. In clay bodies, it promotes vitrification with other materials and reduces shrinkage and warping. In glazes, flint combines with fluxes to promote glaze melting.

flocking – small, colored fibers sprayed on an adhesive-coated ceramic surface

flux – a material that promotes melting

free silica – chemically uncombined silica found in clays and glaze materials

frit – a combination of alumina, silica, calcium, sodium, or other oxides that have been mixed in specific amounts, fired to a glass, fast-cooled, and ground into a powder. Frequently used in low-temperature glazes as a melting agent.

G-200 – potassium-based feldspar used in a clay body formula for its high-temperature fluxing ability. In glazes it is a primary, high-temperature flux, bringing other glaze materials into a melt.

Gerstley borate – an unprocessed soluble ore containing calcium and boron used as a flux in low- to medium-temperature glazes. (It is no longer mined, and stocks are being depleted.)

glaze maturity range – the temperature range in which a glaze stabilizes

goldart stoneware clay – a medium platelet-sized, plastic clay chosen for clay bodies because of its particle size

grog – a calcined, high-temperature alumina silicate that is inert and reduces shrinkage and warping in a clay body. High percentages of grog in a clay body can reduce plasticity.

grolleg kaolin – a primary, high-temperature, white clay used in clay bodies for its white color and particle size. In glazes, it contributes suspension properties, alumina, and silica.

hand building – the forming process of using slabs, coils, extrusions, or pinching to manipulate clay

Hawthorn bond fireclay – a coarse, refractory clay formed against seams of coal, lignite, and other impurities. Used in clay bodies for its "tooth," or ability to stand up in the moist clay-forming operations.

Helmer kaolin – a white firing, high-temperature clay formed on site and used in clay bodies for its refractory qualities and white color. Can be used in slip applications for its ability to flash with brown highlights.

high coefficient of expansion – ceramic materials that, when heated, have a high degree of contraction

hydrocarbon-based fuels – fuel sources including oil, propane, natural gas, wood, sawdust, coal, or any other combustible material

jelly roll lamination – the circular pattern of moist clay when it is extruded from a pug mill

jigger/jollying – a machine that uses a template with a profile and spinning wheel to form moist clay

kiln – an insulated, heated container for the firing of ceramic objects

Kentucky ball clay OM #4 – a small platelet-sized clay used in clay bodies for its plasticity and strength. Used in glazes for its alumina and silica content and ability to keep glazes in suspension.

Kentucky ball clay #9 – a slightly darker firing ball clay than Kentucky ball clay OM #4 with the same plasticity and glaze suspension properties

leather-hard – a stage in drying when clay is cold to the touch, damp, and slightly pliable

lizella stoneware – a high-iron content stoneware clay that can supply brown to tan colors to clay bodies.

lime pop – a clay body defect caused by nodules of lime expanding, due to hydration

low coefficient of expansion – ceramic materials that, when heated, have a low degree of contraction

L.O.I. – Loss On Ignition, the amount of weight lost when ceramic materials are heated to a high temperature

luster glaze – a thin, metallic film, such as gold, silver, or platinum, that coats a ceramic surface

M44 ball clay – a plastic clay used in clay body formulas and glazes because it aids in suspension and supplies alumina and silica to glazes

Mason stain Naples Yellow #6405 – a calcined mixture of iron, silica praseodymium oxide, and zinc oxide

Mason stain Bermuda Green #6242 – a calcined mixture of silica, praseodymium oxide, zinc oxide, and Vanadium Pentoxide used to color glazes

Mason stain Crimson #6003 – a calcined mixture of chromium oxide and zinc used to color glazes

Mason stain Black #6600 – a calcined mixture of cobalt oxide, chromium oxide, iron, and nickel oxide used to color glazes

manganese dioxide powder – can be an active flux; produces weak brown, violet, purple, or red tints in glazes

mechanical water – uncombined water found in ceramic materials that is removed in the first stages of firing. Also called free water.

mesh size – the open spaces in a screen sieve. The larger the mesh size, the finer the particle size.

metallic coloring oxide – cobalt, chrome, iron, rutile, nickel, manganese, copper oxides, or their carbonate equivalents; used to impart color to glazes

micron – unit of measurement; 1 micron equals 1/24,500 of an inch

nepheline syenite – a sodium-based feldspar used as a flux in clay bodies and glazes

neutral atmosphere – can occur in any hydrocarbon-fueled kiln when equal amounts of air and fuel are introduced into the firing chamber

Newman red – a high-iron content stoneware clay that imparts color to clay bodies

nickel carbonate green – a refractory, metallic coloring carbonate that produces a varied array of subtle colors, depending on the base glaze formula, firing temperature, and kiln atmosphere. It is often used to modify and tone down other coloring oxides.

nodule – a small mass of rounded or irregularly shaped particles

ocmulgee stoneware clay – a high-iron content clay used in low-, medium-, and high-temperature clay bodies to produce orange/red colors

orange peel – a dimpled pattern appearing on salt or soda glaze pottery that results from sodium vapors reacting with the alumina and silica in the unglazed clay body

oxidation atmosphere – in hydrocarbon-fueled kilns, the combustion takes place with a higher air-to-fuel ratio

pH – a scale measuring alkalinity and acidity. No. 7 indicates neutrality; lower numbers indicate increased acidity, and higher numbers indicate increased alkalinity.

pin hole – a small, round hole with a smooth edge found in an unfired or fired glaze

Pine Lake fireclay – a plastic fireclay used in clay bodies that is no longer available

Pioneer kaolin – a primary, high-temperature, white clay used in clay bodies for its white color and particle size. In glazes, it contributes suspension properties, alumina, and silica.

pit firing – a firing method in which pottery is fired in a hole in the ground that is enclosed and covered by a combustible material

platelet – a flat structure observable when clay is placed under magnification

porcelain – a white, various clay body that is translucent when thin

primary clay – clay formed by weathering down; not transported from the site or origin

pug mill – a machine with auger blades that compresses the clay into an extruded form

ram press – a hydraulic press in which air is injected into a plaster mold to release the ceramic form

raku – a fast-firing procedure in which the ware is heated, taken out of the kiln when still hot, and placed in a reduction medium or left to cool in an oxidation condition. Either atmosphere can alter a clay body's color and texture.

Redart – a high-iron content earthenware clay used in clay bodies

red iron oxide – one of the most versatile coloring oxides used in glaze formulas; occasionally added to clay bodies for its color effects.

reduction atmosphere – in hydrocarbon-fueled kilns, combustion takes place with a higher fuel-to-air ratio, creating carbon monoxide.

refractory – capable of resisting high temperature

rib – a shape used in clay forming operations; commonly made out of wood or metal

Roseville stoneware clay – a medium-platelet-sized, plastic clay frequently used in clay body formulas for its particle size

rutile powdered light – an ore containing iron and titanium used in glazes to produce weak straw colors, tans, blues, and mottled surface textures

"S" – a crack in the bone-dry, bisque, or fired ware on the floor of the pots. Found in wheel-thrown forms that have not been correctly "coned" during centering

salt firing – Firing process in which sodium chloride is placed into a firing kiln, creating sodium, hydrochloric acid, and chlorine vapor. The sodium vapor reacts with alumina and silica in the clay body, forming a sodium, alumina, silicate glaze.

secondary clay – clay that has been moved from its origin by wind, rain, or moving water

Sheffield clay – a high-iron content earthenware clay producing brown tones in clay bodies

shivering – sheet-like plates of fired glaze that peel off the clay body; caused by the glaze cooling under extreme compression

shrapnel effect – small pieces of clay that explode in the first stage of bisque firing, due to the fast release of steam trapped in the clay body

silica – silicon dioxide, also referred to as flint, is found in all clay bodies and glazes. By itself, it is very refractory and does not melt below 3,110°F (1,710°C).

silica sand F-65 48x – a coarse mesh size of silica used to cut shrinkage and warping in clay body formulas. Also used to promote an "orange peel" effect in soda/salt firing bodies

slip – liquid clay that can be colored with metallic coloring oxides or stains and applied to the ware in the leather-hard, bone-dry, or bisque stages. The term encompasses any combination of materials in a liquid form that can be applied to clay.

slip casting – the process of pouring liquid clay into a mold

slump – deformation of a ceramic form

soda ash – sodium carbonate used in vapor kiln firings. In glazes, it acts as a low-temperature flux and is soluble.

soda firing – sodium carbonate or sodium bicarbonate is placed into a firing kiln, which creates sodium vapors and carbon dioxide. The sodium vapor reacts with alumina and silica in the clay body, forming a sodium, alumina, silicate glaze.

soluble salts – raw material of chlorides, sulfates, silicates of lime, soda, potash, or magnesia that migrate to the surface of a glaze or clay body, causing efflorescence

spraying – a method of glaze application in which atomized glaze is deposited onto a ceramic form by a compressed stream of air from a glaze container

spray booth – an enclosed structure that traps and captures any over-glaze deposited on the ware from a spray gun

stains – commercially prepared mixtures of metallic coloring oxides and stabilizers that have been calcined and ground into a fine powder. They can impart a stable color to glazes or clay bodies often not attainable with just the use of metallic coloring oxides.

stoneware clay – a secondary clay that is semi-plastic and refractory.

strontium carbonate – comparable to other alkaline earth materials such as calcium and barium, it causes opacity in glazes.

superpax – a zirconium silicate used in glaze for opacity

Taylor ball clay – a light-firing clay used in clay bodies for its plasticity. In glazes, it contributes suspension properties, alumina, and silica.

Tennessee ball clay #1 – a light-firing, coarse-grained clay used in clay bodies for its plasticity. In glazes, it contributes suspension properties, alumina, and silica.

Tennessee ball clay #9 – a plastic ball clay used in clay bodies for its plasticity. In glazes, it contributes suspension properties, alumina, and silica.

Tennessee ball clay #10 – a low-organic, medium-grained, white-firing ball clay used in clay bodies for its plasticity. In glazes, it contributes suspension properties, alumina, and silica.

terra sigillata – fine particles of clay applied to low-temperature pottery to produce a smooth, burnished, or rough surface in the fired state.

Texas talc – can be used in glazes where magnesia and silica are needed. In high-temperature clay bodies, talc can be an aggressive flux. In low-temperature clay bodies, it can promote glaze fit.

thermal mass – solid objects that will capture and retain heat, such as kiln shelves, pots, posts, and kiln walls. Upon cooling, objects radiate heat to the surrounding area.

thermal shock – a drastic change in the temperature of a ceramic body

Tile #6 kaolin – a plastic, white-firing, refractory, high-temperature clay used in clay bodies. In glazes, it contributes suspension properties, alumina, and silica.

titanium dioxide – a material that can cause opacity in glazes and in some instances, depending on the cooling cycle in the kiln, produce crystals

tooth – the ability of moist clay to maintain its vertical position in any forming process due to the combination of clay platelet sizes and grog particles

throwing – the process of forming moist clay on the potter's wheel

Thomas ball clay – small-platelet-sized clay that can be used in a clay body for its plastic properties. In glazes, it contributes alumina and silica while aiding in suspension.

tin oxide – an opacity-producing oxide used in glazes

viscosity – a liquid's resistance to flow. A casting slip with a high viscosity will be stiff and move slowly when poured. Low-viscosity casting slips are very fluid and fast-moving when poured.

vitreous – the formation of a glass structure in a clay body due to heating

wedging – the process of hand-kneading the moist clay to distribute moisture and remove air pockets

XX Sagger – a type of ball clay that contributes plastic properties to clay bodies. In glazes, it supplies alumina and silica, while improving suspension properties.

whiting (calcium carbonate) – a finely ground powder used as a source of calcium in glazes.

zinc oxide – acts as a flux in medium- to high-temperature glazes. Contributes to fired glaze hardness and promotes intense blues from cobalt oxide.

Resources

Learning technical information, techniques, and how other potters accomplish their ceramics goals will help you perfect your craft. Listed are several books and magazines that will help potters at all skill levels. Also included are ceramic supply companies that sell clay, glazes, raw materials, equipment, tools, kilns, and other supplies that are useful when making pottery.

Ceramics Supply Companies

Aardvark Clay & Supplies
1400 E. Pomona St.
Santa Ana, CA 92705
714.541.4157
www.aardvarkclay.com

Aardvark Clay & Supplies
6230 Greyhound Ln. #E
Las Vegas, NV 89122
702.451.9898

American Ceramic Supply Co.
2442 Ludelle St.
Fort Worth, TX 76105
817.535.2651
www.americanceramics.com

Axner Pottery Supply
490 Kane Ct.
Oviedo, FL 32765
800.843.7057
407.365.2600
www.axner.com

Bailey Pottery Equipment Corporation
P.O. Box 1577
62 Tenbroeck Ave.
Kingston, NY 12402
800.431.6067
845.339.3721
www.baileypottery.com

Bracker's Good Earth Clays
1831 E 1450 Road
Lawrence, KS 66044
888.822.1982
785.841.4750
www.brackers.com

Ceramic Supply
7 Route 46 West
Lodi, NJ 07644
800.723.7264
973.340.3005
www.7ceramic.com

Continental Clay Co.
1101 Stinson Blvd. NE
Minneapolis, MN 55413
800.432.CLAY
612.331.9332
www.continentalclay.com

Davens Ceramics Center
5076 Peachtree Road
Atlanta, GA 30341
800.695.4805
770.451.2105
www.davensceramiccenter.com

Flat Rock Clay Supplies
2002 S. School Ave.
Fayetteville, AR 72701
479.521.3181
www.flatrockclay.com

Great Lakes Clay & Supply
120 S. Lincoln Ave.
Carpentersville, IL 60110
800.258.8796
www.greatclay.com

Kickwheel Pottery Supply, Inc.
1986 Tucker Industrial Rd.
Tucker, GA 30084
800.241.1895
770.986.9011
www.kickwheel.com

Laguna Clay Company
14400 Lomitas Ave.
City of Industry, CA 91746
626.330.0631
800.452.4862
www.lagunaclay.com

Minnesota Ceramic Supply
962 Arcade St.
St. Paul, MN 55106
800.652.9724
651.774.7007
www.mnceramic.com

Northeast Ceramic Supply, Inc.
621 River St. Ste. 1
Troy, NY 12180
518.274.2722

Pottery Crafts, Ltd.
Campbell Rd.
Stoke-on-Trent
ST4 4ET
Staffordshire, UK
+44.(0)1782.745000
www.potterycrafts.co.uk

Scarva Pottery Supplies
Unit 20 Scarva Road Industrial Estate
Banbridge, Co. Down
Northern Ireland
BT32 3QD
0.(044).28.406.69699
www.scarvapottery.com

Seattle Pottery Supply
35 S. Hanford St.
Seattle, WA 98134
800.522.1975
206.587.0570
www.SeattlePotterySupply.com

Sheffield Pottery, Inc.
995 N. Main St.
P.O. Box 399
Sheffield, MA 01257
888.774.2529
413.229.7700
www.sheffield-pottery.com

Southern Pottery Equipment & Supply
2721 West Perdue
Baton Rouge, LA 70814
225.932.9457
888.503.2299
www.alligatorclay.com

Standard Ceramic Supply Company
P.O. Box 16240
Pittsburgh, PA 15242
412.276.6333
www.standardceramic.com

Trinity Ceramic Supply
9016 Diplomacy Row
Dallas, TX 75247
214.631.0540
www.trinityceramic.com

Tucker's Pottery Supplies, Inc.
15 W. Pearce St. Unit 7
Richmond Hill, ON
L4B 1H6, Canada
800.304.6185
905.889.7705
www.tuckerspottery.com

Ward Burner Systems
P.O. Box 1086
Dandridge, TN 37725
865.397.2914
www.wardburner.com

Periodicals

Ceramics Monthly
P.O. Box 6102
Westerville, OH 43086-6102
www.ceramicsmonthly.org

Pottery Making Illustrated
The American Ceramic Society
735 Ceramic Place
Westerville, OH 43018
www.potterymaking.org

Studio Potter
P.O. Box 352
Manchester, NH 03105
603.325.0759
www.studiopotter.org

Ceramics TECHNICAL
35 William St.
Paddington
Sydney, NSW 2021
Australia

American Ceramics
9 East 45th St.
New York, NY 10017

Books on Ceramics

Berensohn, Paulus. *Finding One's Way with Clay: Pinched Pottery and the Color of Clay.* New York: Simon & Schuster, 1972.

Branfman, Steven. *The Potter's Professional Handbook.* Westerville, OH: The American Ceramic Society, 1999.

Eppler, Richard A. and Douglas R. Eppler. *Glazes and Glass Coatings.* Westerville, OH: The American Ceramic Society, 2000.

Hamer, Frank, and Janet Hamer. *The Potter's Dictionary of Material and Techniques, Fourth Edition.* Philadelphia: A&C Black, 1997.

Hesselberth, John, and Ron Roy. *Mastering Cone 6 Glazes.* Brighton, Ontario: The Glaze Master Press, 2002.

Lawrence.W.G., *Ceramic Science for the Potter.* Philadelphia: Chilton Book Company, 1972.

McColm, Ian J. *Dictionary of Ceramic Science and Engineering, Second Edition.* New York: Plenum Press, 1994.

Parmelee, Cullen W. *Ceramic Glazes, Third Edition.* Boston, MA: Cahners Books, 1972.

Rhodes, Daniel. *Clay and Glazes for the Potter, Third Edition.* Iola, WI: Krause Publications, 2000. Revised and expanded by Robin Hopper.

Zamek, Jeff. *What Every Potter Should Know.* Southampton, MA: Jeff Zamek/Ceramics Consulting Services, 1999.

Zamek, Jeff. *Safety in the Ceramics Studio.* Southampton, MA: Jeff Zamek/Ceramics Consulting Services, 2002.

For a comprehensive listing of ceramics books contact:

The Potter's Shop
31 Thorpe Rd.
Needham, MA 02494
781.449.7687
pottersshop@aol.com
www.thepottersshop.blogspot.com

Glaze Calculation Software

HyperGlaze
Richard Burkett
6354 Lorca Dr.
San Diego, CA 92115
www.hyperglaze.com

Insight
Interactive Ceramic Calculations
1595 Southview Dr. SE
Medicine Hat, AB
T1B 0A1 Canada
406.662.0136
www.digitalfire.com

Glaze Master
Frog Pond Pottery
P.O. Box 88
Pocopson, PA 19366
www.masteringglazes.com

Author's Recent Bibliography

"Pottery Tool Kit," *Pottery Making Illustrated*, November/December 2008.

"Pottery Myths: The Dead Burned-Up Alfred Dog Myth," *The Studio Potter*, Vol. 36, No. 2, Summer 2008.

"Pottery Myths," *Pottery Production Practices*, March 2008.

"Diagnosing Glaze Blister," 4-part series of blog articles on *Pottery Production Practices Magazine* website, February 2008.

"The Economies of Pottery Production," blog article on *Pottery Production Practices Magazine* website, February 2008.

"Talc and Asbestos: What We Know and What We Don't," *Ceramics Monthly*, February 2008.

"Putting the Fire in Clay," *Pottery Production Practices*, September 2007.

"Mixing it Up," *Pottery Production Practices*, September 2007.

"Raku Color and Opacity," *Pottery Making Illustrated*, July/August 2007.

"Surviving the Cold – Calculating Clay Body Absorption," *Pottery Making Illustrated*, May/June 2007.

"A Cautionary Tale," *Pottery Production Practices*, March 2007.

"Curing Lime Pops," *Pottery Making Illustrated*, March/April2007.

"Covering Your Bases," *Pottery Making Illustrated*, November/December 2006.

"Feldspars We Use," "Glazes: Materials, Mixing, Testing and Firing," "Choosing the Right Clay," and "Clays We Use," *2007 Buyers Guide, A Studio Reference*, American Ceramics Society, 2007.

"Ergonomic Rib Tools," *Pottery Production Practices*, September 2006.

"Color and Texture with Engobes," *Pottery Making Illustrated*, September/October 2006.

"6 Steps to Stop Glaze Shivering," *Pottery Making Illustrated*, July/August 2006.

"No More Albany Slip, No More Barnard/Blackbird," *Ceramics Technical*, May-October 2006.

"Eight Steps to Stop Crazing," *Pottery Making Illustrated*, May/June 2006.

"Tools of the Trade," *Pottery Making Illustrated*, March/April 2006.

"Stoneware Clay Body Formulas, Part 2," *Pottery Production Practices*, October 2005.

"Mixing Glazes," *Pottery Making Illustrated*, September/October 2005.

"The Line on Liner Glazes," *Pottery Making Illustrated*, July/August 2005.

"Stoneware Clay Body Formulas, Part 1," *Pottery Production Practices*, June 2005.

"Mix Your Own Clay Body," *Pottery Making Illustrated*, May/June 2005.

"Questioning Cobalt," *Ceramic Industry*, March 2005.

"Tools of the Trade," *Pottery Production Practices*, March 2005.

"Glazes: Materials, Mixing, Testing and Firing," *Ceramics Monthly*, March 2005.

"Choosing the Right Clay," *Ceramics Monthly*, January 2005.

"Substitutes for Gerstley Borate," *Advanced Raku Techniques*, Ceramics Monthly Publisher, 2004.

Suggestions Column, *Ceramics Monthly*, September 2004.

"Clay: An Ongoing Process," *Clay Times*, July/August 2004.

"Cobalt on Trial," *Ceramics Monthly*, June/July/August 2004.

"The Business of Pottery," *Pottery Production Practices*, March 2004.

"Kiln Disasters – Adventures in Graduate School," *Studio Potter* newsletter, Vol. 16, No.1, 2004.

"Using Studio Space to Increase Profits," *Ceramics Monthly*, March 2004.

"Economic Factors and Potters," Yakimono Corporation publication, Minato-ku, Tokyo, Japan , February 2004.

"Studio Practices, Techniques, and Tips," *Ceramics Monthly Handbook*, The American Ceramics Society, 2004.

"Experimenting with Color," *Pottery Production Practices*, December 2003.

Questions Column, *Ceramics Monthly*, December 2003.

"How to Interpret a Typical Data Sheet," *Ceramics Monthly*, November 2003.

"Clay Body Shrinkage & Absorption," *Potter Production Practices*, Summer 2003.

"Identifying and Correcting Clay Body Defects," *Pottery Production Practices*, Spring 2003.

"Clay Body Absorption and Shrinkage," *Ceramics Monthly*, April 2003.

"No More Gerstley Borate," *Exploring Electric Kiln Techniques* The American Ceramic Society, January 2003.

"Influences on Clay Color," *Pottery Production Practices*, Winter 2002.

"Black Clay," *Pottery Making Illustrated*, November/December 2002.

"Managing Raw Material Variability," *Pottery Production Practices*, Fall 2002.

"Continuous Education," *Pottery Making Illustrated*, September/October 2002.

"Safety First: Gloves for the Studio," *Pottery Making Illustrated*, September/October 2002.

Safety in the Ceramics Studio, Krause, August 2002.

"Adjusting Glazes for Color and Opacity," *Ceramic Industry Magazine*, December 2001.

Suggestions Column, *Ceramics Monthly*, December 2001.

"The Potter's Health & Safety Questionnaire," National Council on Education for the Ceramic Arts newsletter, Fall 2001.

"Substitutions for Gerstley Borate," *Ceramics Monthly*, October 2001.

"Additives for Clay Bodies," *Ceramics Industry Magazine*, September 2001.

Suggestions Column, *Ceramics Monthly*, June/July/August 2001.

"Black Friday," *Ceramics Monthly*, May 2001.

"Opening Doors," *Ceramics Monthly*, April 2001.

"The Economics of Raw Materials," *Ceramic Industry Magazine*, March 2001.

"Solutions for Common Health and Safety Issues in the Ceramics Studio," *The Crafts Report*, January 2001.

Index

About the Author

Jeff Zamek walked into a studio 36 years ago and started his career as a potter. After completing a degree in business from Monmouth University in New Jersey, he acquired BFA/MFA degrees in ceramics from Alfred University in New York. While at Alfred he developed the soda-firing system at the college and went on to teach at Simon's Rock College and Keane College. In 1980, he started Ceramics Consulting Services, through which he offers technical advice on clays, glazes, kilns, raw materials, ceramic toxicology, and product development for individuals, companies, and the greater industry. His clay body formulas are presently used in the pottery industry.

Zamek is a regular contributor to *Ceramics Monthly, Pottery Making Illustrated, Pottery Production Practices, Clay Times, Studio Potter, Ceramics Technical,* and *Craft Horizons.* He is the author of *What Every Potter Should Know* (Krause, 1999) and *Safety in the Ceramics Studio* (Krause, 2002). He lives in Southampton, Massachusetts.

For more information,
Jeff Zamek can be contacted at:
Ceramics Consulting Services
6 Glendale Woods Drive, Southampton, MA 01073
(413) 527-7337
fixpots@aol.com
www.fixpots.com

Acknowledgments

I would like to thank Jim Fineman, a professional potter, who has for the past ten years been my technical editor. Jim works in clay every day and understands the requirements of potters with all levels of experience. He always has the needs of the audience in mind.

One of the many advantages of working with clay is the opportunity to meet people who have the same love of the craft. Steven Branfman, a good friend, professional potter, lecturer, and raku expert, has always given me excellent advice on writing and publishing.

Jim Bailey, President of Bailey Pottery Equipment Corporation, has supplied several images for this book. His pottery equipment designs set the standard for ceramics. John Cowen, president of Sheffield Pottery, Inc., and John Benedict at Sheffield have inspired ceramics research and writing.

Jim Turnbull, President of Ceramic Supply of New York/New Jersey, is always supportive and informative when I report on developments in the field.

Tom White, professional potter, generously offered kiln space for pottery featured in this book.

Kristin Muller, director of the ceramics program at the Brookfield Craft Center, was instrumental in finding me a good home at Quarry Books.

Professional potters Chuck Stern, Hiroshi Nakayama, Dennis Bern, Oliver Greene, Emily Pearlman, Richard Buncamper, Michael Cohen, and Angela Fina have generously donated images of their pottery, advice, and encouragement.

Thank you to The Artisan Gallery (162 Main Street, Northampton, MA 01060, (413) 586-1942, www.TheArtisanGallery.com), which graciously allowed us to photograph their pottery gallery.

I would like to thank the staff at Quarry Books and their freelancers who have given my book a higher level of professional care than I could have imagined when I started to write years ago: Rochelle Bourgault, Acquisitions Editor; Kristen Hampshire, Developmental Editor; Tiffany Hill, Project Manager; Jennifer Bright Reich, Copy Editor; Rosalind Loeb Wanke, Creative Director; David Martinell, Art Director; and Randy O' Rouke, photographer.

I would like to acknowledge Val Cushing, who set the standard for my research in the field of ceramics.